BEING CATHOLIC NOW

BEING CATHOLIC NOW

PROMINENT AMERICANS TALK
ABOUT CHANGE IN THE CHURCH
AND THE QUEST FOR MEANING

KERRY KENNEDY

 CROWN PUBLISHERS · NEW YORK

Published in the United States by the Crown Publishing Group,
a division of Random House, Inc., New York.
www.crownpublishing.com

Crown is a trademark and the Crown colophon is a registered
trademark of Random House, Inc.

Library of Congress Cataloging-in-Publication Data
Kennedy, Kerry.
    Being Catholic now: prominent Americans talk about change in
the church and the quest for meaning / Kerry Kennedy.—1st ed.
        1. Catholic Church—United States. 2. Church renewal—Catholic
Church. 3. Catholics—Religious life—United States. 4. Catholics—
United States—Interviews. I. Title.
    BX1406.3.C86   2008
    282.092'273—dc22   2008000520

ISBN 978-0-307-34684-1

Printed in the United States of America

DESIGN BY BARBARA STURMAN

10 9 8 7 6 5 4 3 2 1

First Edition

For my mother—
     Ethel Skakel Kennedy;

My children—
     Cara, Mariah, and Michaela;

My godchildren—
     Rory, Kat, Matt, Kyra, Kerry,
     Catie, and Harrison;

and

All God's Children

Contents

Acknowledgments

First and foremost, I want to thank all the Catholics who took the time to speak with me about a subject that is deeply personal and who did so with raw honesty and integrity of spirit. Thank you to my agent, David Kuhn, who suggested the idea of writing this book, and to Abigail Pogrebin, whose book *Stars of David*, about being Jewish, inspired this one. Read it! Gabrielle Fox and Jack Downey researched the subjects and David Timothy, Matthew Smith, and Amy Bowden transcribed the tapes at lightning speed. Thank you most especially to Emily Liebert, who suggested revisions on the manuscript, checked my work, made considerable improvements, and then did it all over again. And again. And again. To Lena Adely, for typing and tracking down releases, photographs, and so much more; to Neil MacFarquhar, who has been a dream; to Nan Richardson, Jill Brooke, Kathleen Kennedy Townsend, Father Charlie Beirne, Tessa Souter, Father Charlie Curry, and and their amazing red pens; to Timothy Shriver for reading the manuscript and offering valuable insights and wisdom about faith and the wonders of Catholicism; and to Charles Stevenson and Alex Kuczynski, who provided ten blissful days on the banks of the Salmon River where much of this was written, thank you. A very special thanks to Rick Horgan, my Random House editor, for his availability and help throughout.

This book, in many ways, has been nearly fifty years in the making, and I want to acknowledge a few of the many people who taught me the true meaning of Catholicism. My very first interview was with Father Robert Drinan. He served in Congress for a decade championing nuclear arms control, criminal justice reform, and the development of international legal norms to protect human rights, and he was the first to call for the impeachment of Richard Nixon. After he continuously defied warnings from the Vatican by voting for anti-poverty legislation (bills that included funding for family planning clinics that offered abortions), Pope John Paul II asked him to resign. Father Joe Hacala ran the Campaign for Human Development, the Church's antipoverty program. I miss him every day. Father Gerry Creedon caused so much trouble advocating on behalf of and raising funds for the poor in his northern Virginia parish that rumor had it he was exiled to the far reaches of the Dominican Republic. Father Charlie Beirne became vice president of the University of Central America in El Salvador after the military assassinated the Jesuits there, and Father Mark Hessian preached from the pulpit about tolerance for all minority groups—racial, religious, and sexual. Father Greg Boyle works with gangs at Homeboy Industries in East Los Angeles. Sister Helen Prejean of New Orleans works to abolish the death penalty, and Father Peter Klink helps Native Americans on the Pine Ridge Reservation in South Dakota. Their colleagues in the struggle for justice include Father Tim Njoya of Kenya, Father Jerzy Popieluszko of Poland, Father Ham of South Korea, Bishop Carlos Felipe Ximenes Belo of East Timor, Archbishop Oscar Romero of El Salvador, Sister Digna Ochoa, Sister Dianna Ortiz, advocate for victims of torture, and Father John Quinn. The list goes on. I have been deeply inspired by these heroes' commitment and capacity to create change against overwhelming odds. All of them found a cause for which they were willing to die, and all seemed, thereby, to have found a reason to live. Their social activism has been and is informed by their Catholic faith.

While the wider world has shown me much about the message of Jesus, the gift of faith was passed on to me primarily by the women in my life. Thank you to my sisters, Kathleen, Courtney, and Rory, and to my best friend, Mary Richardson Kennedy.

Three women have exemplified for me the Catholic mainstays of faith, hope, and charity. Thank you to Rose Kennedy for her unwavering belief, Ena Bernard for her sense of fun and optimism, and my mother, Ethel, for her boundless heart.

"No one has ever seen God. Yet if we love one another, God dwells in us, and his love is brought to perfection in us" (1 John 4:12). Thank you, most of all, to my daughters, Cara, Mariah, and Michaela, whose infinite love reveals a glimpse of the Almighty.

Introduction

I was in Rome on the night that I received the happy news that Random House would publish this book exploring what it means to be a Catholic. Twelve hours later I was shaking hands with Pope Benedict XVI. I had mixed feelings about meeting the Holy Father, who, as the leader of a billion Catholics worldwide, represented all I have come to love and admire about the Catholic Church. Still, there was much about the new pope that gave me pause. Part of my ambiguity could be traced to the very reason I was in Rome in the first place. I had been invited to chair a panel for the annual meeting of Nobel Peace Prize laureates. They had gathered for a conference on Africa, where an estimated thirty million people are projected to die of AIDS by the year 2020, a number that would be drastically reduced by strong preventive measures including widespread condom use. A word from the Church and millions of lives could be saved.

Before becoming pope, Cardinal Ratzinger was a staunch defender of the magisterium of the Catholic Church, which holds that the use of birth control is a mortal sin and therefore that couples who use condoms may be condemning themselves to eternal damnation. As prefect of the Congregation for the Doctrine of the Faith, he had also silenced advocates of liberation theology, attacked those who advanced a more progressive stance on homosexuality, and declared secret the details of Church investigations into accusations made against priests of certain serious ecclesiastical crimes, including sexual abuse. When the Holy Father approached me, I asked, "Your Eminence, in view of the tragedy unfolding in Africa, for the sake of the sanctity of life, would you consider changing the Church's position on the use of condoms?" I don't know if the devout Catholic to my left was more horrified or terrified, but upon hearing my plea, she leaped backward, rattling the multitude of St. Christopher medals and rosary beads she'd brought along in hopes of attaining his blessing. Apparently, she feared I'd be struck dead right then and there and she wanted to get as far away from me as possible, just in case the lightning bolt missed its target. Meanwhile, the pope gazed beneficently, imparting "God bless you" as he passed.

From that encounter I embarked on an intensive period of interviews, ultimately focusing on how thirty-seven American Catholics interpret their faith. I set out to speak with Catholics who were well known for depth and expertise on a particular issue or profession and who represented different walks of life—actors, historians, journalists, commentators, political figures, educators, judges, cardinals, priests, nuns, union leaders, doctors, activists, comedians, businessmen, and students. They range in age from nineteen to eighty-six; they are white, Latino, and African American; they are liberal and conservative, women and men; they embody the old order and the harbingers of what's to come. They include those who love the Church and those who feel the Church wronged them. Some have left, others have come back, some work for change, and still others have devoted their lives to upholding the institution as it is. Most are lifelong Catholics, one is a midlife convert from Judaism to Catholicism, and another is a convert from Catholicism to Islam.

Looking back, that thirty-second encounter with the Roman pontiff echoed the dilemma with which almost every Catholic I interviewed grapples. On the one hand, there is the ingrained principle that members of the hierarchy—the pope, the cardinals, the bishops, and the priests—are the direct conduits between the laity and God. As such, these men are regarded with respect, sometimes even awe, and are bestowed a generous portion of the benefit of the doubt. Thus there is an instinctive reaction against questioning their judgment, not to mention their supremacy. On the other hand, few would deny that some of what the Catholic Church teaches, and sometimes the manner in which it conducts itself, is at odds with the very values Catholics are taught that Jesus preached. Speaking truth to power is a strong tradition in the Catholic faith, starting with the Savior himself challenging the Pharisees and the Jewish authorities. But the message has always been mixed, as Catholics are taught both obedience to authority and to venerate saints who challenged the status quo.

I found that those raised in the pre–Vatican II Church voiced aggravation either with the changes they've seen or with the promise of change that remains unfulfilled. Those who came of age post–Vatican II are unshaken by the failures of the hierarchy because they never developed expectations about the integrity of institutions, having begun their political awareness during or after the Watergate era and having witnessed two presidents facing impeachment; the financial scandals of the savings and loans; WorldCom and Enron; the mortgage crisis; the betting and steroids scandals in the sports world; and the pedophile scandals in the Church.

But what quickly became apparent during the interviews, was the distinction Catholics are able to make between their personal spiritual journeys and their varying attitudes toward the Institutional Church. Criticism of the Church is a heartfelt concern, but rarely is it an obstacle to a deep sense of faith, a strong connection to the community, and a firm commitment to carrying forward the message of Jesus in one's daily life. Even those who've left the Church agreed to be interviewed for a book about being Catholic. This speaks to the undeniable force with which the Catholic faith penetrates to the bones and endures. Its message of social justice, piety, prayer, spirituality, and intellectual curiosity stays with Catholics throughout their lives, regardless of whether they attend services or agree with the pope. The old adage "Once a Catholic, always a Catholic" rings true. The word "Catholic" is from the Greek *catolica*, meaning "universal," and when seemingly disparate voices can all declare, "I'm a Catholic," they are acknowledging their part of the universal, the whole. We're all one. At the end of the day, that is the consistent message of faith.

What comes across in these stories is that the Church is, by definition, full of contradictions—Jesus has come but is still coming; Jesus is divine but fully human; Jesus died but rose from the dead; Jesus saved the world but the world needs to be saved; the Church is the bride of Christ and also the mystical body of Christ. The Church has always embraced conflict and contradiction. Ask two theologians about the Church and one will portray the triumphalism of the Church—its glory, its majesty, its divinity, its rich history—while another will proclaim the poverty of the Church—its need to pursue social justice, its missionary role to aid the excluded. When parishioners wonder what that all means, they're told, "Mass is over, go in peace." The Catholic laity says, "I don't get all these conflicting messages," and the hierarchy responds, "Yes, you don't get it, but that's our faith."

Perhaps that's a source of strength, as Catholics then can feel comfortable with other areas of life where conflict is inherent. In the midst of agonizing loss, there's a sudden openness; in the midst of euphoric love, there is overwhelming fear; in the midst of rage over injustice, there's the possibility of revolutionary change. It's common for conflicting emotions to coexist, and the Catholic approach allows for both to be held in one's hands at the same time. And yet Catholics are profoundly disturbed.

Generations ago, the search for spirituality came predefined and prepackaged. The Baltimore Catechism not only gave us all the answers, it even gave us the questions to ask. Now all that packaging has been subjected to criticism and has been found wanting. Religion today is at a time of enormous change. When addressing such issues as immigration, the mishandling of the pedophile crisis, the notion of a just war in the post–9/11 world, the suppression of women, the intolerance of homosexuality, birth control, abortion, euthanasia, stem cell research, along with a host of other issues that Anna Quindlen defines as "gynecological theology," Catholics express anguish, disappointment, frustration, anger, and despair. As a result, some have left the Church altogether, some simply dismiss the hierarchy, and others work for change. We're all in a boat that has been rocked. Everyone is struggling to find the proper balance; for comfort, for truth. I hope this constellation of voices will add a bit of much-needed ballast.

Each person's journey within the faith is her or his own. Religion is an intensely personal, deeply felt system of beliefs. It's rooted in history, in conviction, in pageantry, in family, and in heritage. It inflects our every action and thought. Religion, at its core, has always been about the search for ultimate meaning. All of us are engaged in that exploration but not always in a conscientious way. The people interviewed in this book face that journey with rare courage. These stories, raw, emotion laden, and honest, give us guideposts with which to conduct our own search for meaning in our quest for spiritual authenticity.

Preface

In the final days of the crucial California primary in the 1968 presidential race, I was traveling on the campaign with my father, mother, and three of my ten brothers and sisters. I was eight years old. We spent the morning at Disneyland, where I was enthralled by the dolls representing the full array of international costumes, singing in unison, "It's a small world after all." The last stop was the souvenir shop, where we passed up the Mickey Mouse ears for the joke gifts. I bought an intricately etched cut-glass tumbler that dribbled its contents on the unsuspecting drinker. Two days later, when my parents and David headed off to the Ambassador Hotel to await the results and the much-anticipated victory party, Courtney, Michael, and I were sent off to bed. The following morning, I awoke early and turned on the television to watch Bugs Bunny. A news flash interrupted the cartoon. That's how I learned my father had been shot.

A few hours later, the astronaut John Glenn, a friend of my parents, came to tell us that it was true. Daddy was lying in a hospital; we couldn't visit him, and it didn't look good. David, Michael, Courtney, and I were whisked back to Hickory Hill, our home in Virginia. Late that same night, our older brother Joe called to say that Daddy had died.

I ran into my room, buried my head in my pillow, and instinctively began to pray. For my father and mother. For our family. And then I remember clearly, praying, "God, don't let them kill the man who killed Daddy."

Preventing vengeance is a mainstay of the Catholic faith, even to an eight-year-old.

By 1968 death had already been visited upon my family with horrifying regularity. By the age of eight, I'd recoiled over and over again, unable to turn the channel or flip the page fast enough as I watched my uncle and my father shot dead. Uncle George was killed in a plane crash, along with my parents' best friend, Dean Markham, a fixture in our household. Ruby Reynolds, the loving woman who lived with us since the time I was born and cooked our meals, had died. My aunts Jackie and Joan gave birth to babies who died before we ever met them. Martin Luther King Jr. died. Putt, the ancient fisherman, deaf, dumb, and beloved, who met us on Great Island off Hyannis Port every day of the summer, also passed away.

We found solace in prayer; only God understood our agony. Each night we prayed to God that he'd bring directly to heaven an ever-growing number of relatives and friends. "Daddy, Grandma and Grandpa Skakel, Grandpa Kennedy, Joe, Kick, Jack, Patrick, Dean, George, Sissy, Vince, Ruby, Putt, Annie . . ." The list grew: Marie, Billy, Peter, Jeff, Michael, David, Lewann, Georgeanne, Pat . . . And grew: Gerry, Spider, Margie, Averell, Lem, Cary, Carol, Vitas, Henry, Lorenzo, Jerzy, Abba, Willy, Carmine, Santina. That litany was a nightly reminder that our loved ones were together in heaven forever and our time on earth is finite.

I watched my parents, then my mother alone, my grandmother, and aunts and uncles sort through the trauma, trying to grapple with their pain while dealing with all of us. The one solace seemed to be prayer. The Catholic Church taught us that all the people we loved so dearly weren't gone forever, but blissfully happy in heaven with angels and God, and that they were never far from us. We'd all be reunited one wonderful day.

Repeating the prayers of the Rosary was transformative, with the chaotic energy of this large family chanting together, and at times, it seemed, we were entering almost a trancelike state of peace. I knew that God understood the anguish I was enduring, the terror and the pain, and the Catholic Church became a kind of a lifeline, the one place that could make sense of all this suffering. Prayer sustained us. We woke up, got on our knees, and consecrated the day to the glory of God through the immaculate heart of Mary. Before breakfast, lunch, and dinner, we gave thanks to Almighty God for the gifts we were about to receive, and then after each meal we thanked God for the food we'd eaten and for the hands that made it. We prayed to St. Anthony for anything that needed to be found, from a cure to world poverty, to the keys or a parking space. We prayed to St. Blaise for our throats, to St. Christopher when the plane took flight, to St. Jude for lost causes, and to St. Francis for our animals. We prayed when we were happy, sad, mourning, angry, scared, or grateful. We prayed at home; in school; at church; and in planes, boats, and cars. We prayed in groups, alone, silently, and aloud. We prayed with memorized prayers and conversationally. We used palms, water, oil, candles, bread, wine, hymns, masses, crucifixes, rosaries, and the St. Christopher medals hanging around each of our necks to help us pray.

We read the Bible aloud every night after dinner, and the Old Testament's stories of God's steadfast support of warriors for justice complemented the New Testament's "Blessed are"s and dictates to love God, love one another, serve the poor, and seek justice. Service to society in general and the poor in particular were sacrosanct. Before sleep, we kneeled around my parents' king-sized bed or on the second-floor landing in front of a radiant crystal crucifix and beneath a framed poster by Sister Corita that read, "To believe in God is to know that the rules will be fair and that there will be wonderful surprises." We prayed to the Lord our souls to keep, for Mary to defend us, and to God to bless our family and make us all good.

In addition to our daily devotions, we participated with gusto in annual rites. We went to Mass on each of the holy days of obligation, as well as on Ash Wednesday. Only Walt Disney could compete with my mother in the total makeover of our home at each holiday. The day after Thanksgiving, while other families hit the malls, our house underwent a complete renovation. By the time the first Sunday of Advent rolled around three days later, and we gathered to say the Rosary and compete over who got to light the first purple candle embedded in a fresh wreath, our center hall colonial had been transformed into eye-popping splendor. A platform held Rudolph, his nose a blinking red bulb, followed by a harness with eight life-sized reindeer. There was Santa in his sleigh riding across the snowy spun-glass draped tops of the English boxwood hedge in front of the house. Electric candles pierced the centers of thirty-six balsam wreaths in the thirty-six windows. Walking through the front door triggered jingle bells, which could be heard over the Bing Crosby and Andy Williams Christmas albums playing 24/7 from Thanksgiving till the Feast of the Epiphany, January 6.

The entrance hall featured fir and pine garlands draped over the front door, over the entrances to the office on the right and the TV room on the left, over the archway straight ahead, and again over the door to the dining room just beyond. The doors to the powder room, kitchen, and living room also had a sprig of green above each, tied with a bright red velvet bow. The center arch featured an enormous sequin-covered ball, with a generous portion of mistletoe tied beneath, rendering it impossible to pass into the house without an obligation to kiss the first person in the line of sight, a source of constant amusement to the younger kids. A golden Santa shimmied up a golden rope hanging from the TV room ceiling. With a bulging sack, Santa also stood five feet tall and turned around and shook hands at the bottom of the stairs. Santa stood in various guises on every table, and, stuffed, on every chair. Electronic versions greeted revelers at every doorway. The three flights of stairs were wrapped and then draped with bows of holly and spruce, tied every eighteen inches or so with a red velvet bow holding a laughing Santa with a soft cotton-ball beard.

Spode Christmas china replaced the usual white, and the entire dining room was converted to Christmas cheer, from the three crèches on three sideboards to the angels and reindeer at the centerpiece to the sudden appearance of ribbon candy and red and white peppermint canes in sterling bowls throughout the first floor. Just before the holidays my mother would file us into the station wagon and take us caroling to homes of elderly and infirm friends. When the Savior was born, the angels announced, "Joy to the world." Indeed, my mother did her best to assure that all of us celebrated his birth with festive delight.

We celebrated Christmas on the Saturday before December 25, and midmorning we headed to the airport for a flight to ski in the Rockies. It wasn't easy to find a home that would accommodate our sizable brood, and one year my mother rented the guest house of a Trappist monastery just outside Aspen. The monks had only recently relaxed the vow of silence, and we spent that vacation skiing all day and then talking with the Trappist brothers about religious life, which they liked, and raising chickens, which most of them, it turned out, abhorred.

What I remember most was the tangible, physical sensation of the inner peace I felt in every ounce of my being when the monks sang madrigals in harmony in their simple brick chapel. That place of simple beauty, stripped bare of distraction, allowed me to empty my heart and mind of every burden and thrill and, in that sublime stillness, to discover a rare serenity, to touch something that felt profound, holy, and full of peace, deep within. It was then that I understood the lure of sacrificing every pleasure for the contemplative life.

After the New Year, the holidays came with soothing regularity, the secular blending seamlessly with the sacred. For St. Valentine's Day the house was similarly transformed to a mass of hearts and angels; on St. Patrick's Day leprechauns and shamrocks turned our home green; and Easter was all bunnies, pastel colors, bright flowers, and baby lambs. These were the decorative manifestations of a deeper faith and a reflection of the call to joy. After forty days of abstinence from chocolate, candy, soda, and ice cream, the girls received matching dresses, new white stockings and gloves, and shiny black patent-leather shoes. We looked forward to Palm Sunday and creating crosses from the palm fronds handed out at church. On Holy Thursday we remembered the Last Supper and quizzed one another about who could identify all the apostles at the table. We had no school on Friday and engaged in great debates about whether Lenten resolutions could be broken Saturday night or had to wait till Sunday morning. We spent much of Saturday dyeing hundreds of Easter eggs, and on Sunday Father Creedon came to say Mass at Hickory Hill. We gathered in the living room along with twenty or thirty Washingtonians to affirm our faith and the righteousness of progressive politics before a massive Easter egg hunt.

On Halloween, we dressed in our costumes immediately after school and headed for Georgetown University Hospital where we visited the infirm and gave out candies to the nurses and the patients alike. We were reminded that this was the eve of All Souls' Day, which St. Patrick transformed from a pagan festival into a Catholic tradition.

Beyond the holidays, there was evidence of our Catholicism throughout Hickory Hill, as if the simple fact of eleven children wasn't enough. Each of the thirteen bedrooms had a holy water font next to the door frame, a cross or a statue of Mary on a table, and a Bible on a shelf, alongside biographies of St. Francis, Joan of Arc, St. Catherine, or St. Patrick, as well as *The Lives of the Saints, God Calling*, and *God at Eventide*. Most of us had sterling crosses, blessed by the pope, hanging above our beds. There was a statue of St. Francis in the boxwood garden at Hickory Hill and one near the herbs in Hyannis Port. A Lucite frame on the bedside table of every room, and another in the kitchen and dining rooms, detailed the Mass schedule at two local churches.

When we were sick, we took St. Joseph aspirin for children. We played Mass and used chalky Necco wafers for hosts.

The front hall closets in both Hyannis Port and at Hickory Hill hosted a huge stack of short, fat, dog-eared black leather missals, brimming with Mass cards. In addition, for the girls there was a ready supply of mantillas, the lace scarves we wore at Mass (white for summer and black for the rest of the year), and an assortment of white gloves, with no guarantee of the correct match, except that the sister who raided the closet earliest on Sunday would probably find a perfect pair, an honor I think I never once merited.

In fourth grade, I transferred from the local Protestant school to join my two older sisters at the Convent of the Sacred Heart. Women were in charge, women whom I came to know, admire, love, and see in leadership roles, an important lesson for a girl in a male-favoring household, religion, and society.

Looking back, the lessons learned at the convent were enduring and valuable. My savior was the Mother Superior; Mother Mouton, a wise Frenchwoman, who, whenever I was sent to her, asked if I was sorry, reminded me that Jesus loved me no matter how I (mis)behaved, gave me a lollipop, and condemned the war in Vietnam. Thus Reverend Mother taught an early lesson in both the wisdom of reconciliation and the importance of political awareness.

My family was also brimming with strong women, all of whom attended the Convent of the Sacred Heart and all of whom consistently impressed us with their unwavering faith, starting with my father's mother, Rose. When we visited Grandma Kennedy's home in Palm Beach, she took us daily to Mass and then quizzed us at the breakfast table about the scripture readings and the content of the sermon. It was a matter of pride to be able to answer her questions correctly and disappointing to fail in her eyes. When she became homebound, a priest came to the house every Sunday, and the extended family gathered in her dining room for services. Mass at home was a common occurrence. The Battersea lace tablecloth we used at lunch the day before, newly washed and ironed, would be draped over a side table that was transformed into the altar. With a wineglass serving as the chalice, cousins leading the psalm response, and each of us chiming in for special intentions, Mass became familiar, comfortable, intimate, warm, and as will be clear in a moment, highly political.

Across two solid decades and more, at least one of us, and usually several, prepared for the sacraments of baptism, First Communion, or confirmation. The Church was simply part of our world, in the same way oxygen is required for breathing.

Throughout it all, my mother found the fire to attend church every day. She took us all with her on Sundays, and—kicking, screaming, and teasing one another—to confession once a month. After my father died, she took us to Mass on Mondays, Wednesdays, and Fridays as well. She went on retreats at the Convent of the Sacred Heart. She met Popes Pius XII, John XXIII, Paul VI, and John Paul II; there are frames scattered throughout the house recording these most auspicious occasions. Her prized possession is the zucchetto given to my parents when they visited Pope John XXIII.

Every May 29, we visited Uncle Jack's grave at Arlington National Cemetery, to remember his birthday, and then eight days later, on June 6, hundreds of old friends and family followed us home from Mass at Arlington, remembering my father's life. We'd each participate in the Mass, reading from scripture, taking up gifts, and singing 1960s folk songs and spirituals. Each reading was carefully chosen for its resonance of the issues Robert Kennedy devoted his life to: peace, justice, tolerance, courage, uplifting the poor, empowering citizens. These themes were so thoroughly interwoven into the readings, the homily, and the conversations with priests that, to me, Catholicism and social justice work were one and the same. Along with Father Pereira or Father Creedon, we returned to the cemetery on November 20, for my father's birthday, and again on November 22 to remember President Kennedy on the day he died.

By any standards, my mother was a devout Catholic, but she laced her unwavering faith with a healthy dose of skepticism directed squarely at the institution of the Church. She loved the pope and the parish priest but had little time for anyone in the hierarchy between. She consistently questioned the priorities of cardinals and bishops who, in her view, too often chose the institution of the Church over the sufferings of the poor. She was highly critical of those who failed to take a forthright stance on the issues of the day—from the war in Vietnam, to Watergate, to nuclear disarmament, to military spending in Central America, to the housing, education, and health issues in the poorest pockets of our own country. She was outraged by any priest who failed to include a prayer for those in the headlines of the latest disaster. She was offended by pomposity, and she demonstrated her impatience with long-winded sermons (anything over ten minutes) by walking out of Mass, followed by her children like so many ducks in a row. My mother was also suspicious of clergy until they passed the poverty test. If they spoke on behalf of, or worked among, the poor, they were invited into the fold. So, from a young age, I learned from her to distinguish between my faith and the Institutional Church.

Catholicism enriched my life, guided my actions, and fed my political belief in the capacity and responsibility to alleviate suffering. Catholicism was integrated into every aspect of my family's intellectual, moral, social, cultural, political, and spiritual life. It was impossible to separate the influence of the Church from that of our Irish heritage or Democratic politics.

But the Catholicism I grew up with isn't the same Catholicism I teach my children, nor is it the same faith I now profess. My relationship with the Church has changed and evolved. I'm still a Catholic, but I'm not the Catholic I once was. I am profoundly disturbed by the problems I see within the Church—in some things it has said, some things it has done, and some things it has failed to do, yet my faith is stronger than ever.

In 1975 I left home for boarding school. The Putney School was situated on a nearly self-sufficient farm in Vermont, where two hundred students worked together. Competition was frowned upon and cooperation was rewarded generously. The daily assemblies, the intellectual rigor, the respect for the earth, the skepticism toward the pecking order, the embrace of political participation, and a decision-making process in which students, teachers, grounds crew, and administration all had a voice fostered a deep sense of communal commitment from which I drew enormous strength and spiritual depth. In fact, the very aspects of Putney I valued most are essential to Catholic faith in practice. My faith remained, but Mass didn't seem particularly relevant to me during those adolescent years and was limited to visits home.

This diminishing relevance was neither a rejection nor a moment of blinding epiphany. It was more subtle. The bonds that had protected me in childhood, which accompanied me through times of joy and celebration as well as sustained me through unimaginable pain and loss, began to loosen. What I didn't know was that those bonds would be severely tested in a series of encounters with the hierarchy of the Church.

In 1977 I left boarding school for college, starting my freshman year at Brown University. There, a dear friend was brutalized and raped. Her anguish and pain are vivid to me even now. With great reservation, she made the journey to Planned Parenthood and ended the pregnancy. Wracked by guilt, she confessed to a priest, who curtly responded, "Do you have any other sins to confess? Murder, perhaps?"

Thirty years later I'm still outraged by that reaction of incomprehensible cruelty. A battered young woman who turned to the Church for mercy, forgiveness, and compassion was instead battered all over again by a callousness no words can define.

Where was the love shown by Christ, a man who had shocked the leading Pharisees of the day when he befriended the ostracized and demanded that the outcasts be invited to the table? The willingness of a priest to pass judgment without regard to the harm caused to the faithful stunned me. I'm pro-choice, but even if I were ardently pro-life my outrage would have been the same. Christ wasn't to be found in the actions of that particular priest.

I hadn't lost faith, but I was skeptical when on April 24, 1984, a student interrupted a lecture I was attending at Boston College Law School to hand me a note. *Call home. Urgent.*

I phoned my mother, who told me that my brother David had died the night before of a drug overdose. The darkness David bravely navigated from addiction to recovery to addiction again was over. The demons had finally won.

My family gathered at Hickory Hill and our longtime family priest, Father Gerry Creedon, comforted us with stories, laughter, and an understanding of the love that we felt deeply for one another at that time of mourning, a time that echoed many times of heartache past and the prologue of more grief to come.

We arrived at Holyhood Cemetery in Brookline to find the newly appointed archbishop Bernard Law and his entourage waiting. The last thing anyone in my family wanted was pomp. What we wanted was Father Creedon, the priest we knew and trusted, to put David to rest. But the archbishop wasn't to be denied, and instead we got a long-winded, dark sermon from a man who hadn't an inkling of who David was. His insertion of rank and insensitivity to a family in mourning left me with the distinct impression that this new archbishop was far more interested in asserting his power than in serving his flock.

I had only one other personal encounter with Law (who was later made a cardinal). When my sister and her fiancé attempted to have their wedding by the sea on Cape Cod, the characteristically authoritarian Law put a halt to the plans, calling outdoor weddings forbidden and instead choosing his man-made building over God's creation as the appropriate place to celebrate the union. The Sermon on the Mount would have been the lecture in the cathedral if Law had had his way. Again, it seemed that asserting authority and maintaining archaic rules were more important to this cardinal than helping a young couple forge their lifelong commitment to love one another.

Sadly, because of encounters like this, and what she sees as the hypocrisy of too many members of the hierarchy, my sister, like many Catholics, feels driven away from the Church.

Others take a more adversarial approach. One friend became increasingly outraged as he endured a sermon that amounted to a frontal assault on gay men's and women's rights. With no small struggle, he had fought through a blizzard to reach the small suburban church that morning, along with his two preschool-aged daughters, two elderly women, and a young, very pregnant Latina housekeeper wearing a wedding band. Afterward my friend confronted the priest. "This is a family Mass. Look around you. No one here is having an abortion. You are completely out of touch with the congregation and you are taking the coward's way out. If you want to rail in Chappaqua, rail against the greed of the rich, the evils of consumerism and waste in the midst of the misery of poverty. At least that would be relevant." That congregant's forthright stance should encourage others to speak up. This is, after all, our Church, and the men running it need feedback, both critical and positive.

When the pedophile scandal made the headlines, it pushed Catholics further away from their faith, but, like many Catholics, I had felt disappointed, angry, and fed up with the Church for a host of reasons long before this injustice.

Too often, when grappling with complex social issues, Church teaching seems insensitive to the complexities of the situation. For example, I understand the Church's ban on euthanasia because of its insistence on the sanctity of all human life. But the latest requirement to provide continuing nourishment even for those in a permanent vegetative state seems extreme. So too do some interpretations of Church teaching on continuing to provide extraordinary means of health care to terminally ill patients seem out of touch with human suffering and the reality of people's lives. The problem is often an overly strict interpretation when a less burdensome interpretation is possible.

The abortion issue, similarly complex, has been met with cold proclamations rather than any attempt to deal with its complexity. Consider my dear friend who was told that the fetus she carried was infected with a virus and was certain to die before birth, and that every day she carried it increased the risks to her health. The Catholic hospital where she was being treated refused to perform the abortion yet told her getting one was imperative. Where is the logic in that? In truth, there is a rich debate within the Church among theologians about these issues, but the public generally only hears the simple answers to complex questions.

Furthermore, the Church loses its moral authority when it gives lip service to values like the dignity of workers but then acts in ways that are clearly antiunion and antilabor. Or when the Church commits to finding ways to empower women while allowing bishops to ban girls from participating in ceremonies. All eyes were on New York in April 2008 when Pope Benedict made his historic visit to Saint Patrick's Cathedral, yet at that highly symbolic moment the Church chose to exclude women from serving as altar servers and ushers at Mass. Catholics and non-Catholics alike are often perplexed about the entire issue of annulment. Try to explain that a civil divorce says that what was once a marriage is no longer a marriage, whereas an annulment says that the marriage never really existed, because the vows were invalid when made, in the eyes of the Church. Almost all annulments applied for in the United States are granted and most of those that are appealed in Rome are denied.

Sometimes these arguments can seem so Byzantine and convoluted that the Church appears out of touch with reality.

The Catholic Church isn't a democracy, and we, as lay Catholics, can't just vote the rascals out. But neither can we allow the Church we love to be abandoned to the dark side. There are many people working for change within the Church, and there are many ways to participate in those changes.

Geoff Boisi started the National Leadership Roundtable on Church Management to promote excellence and best practices in the management, finances, and human resources development of the Catholic Church in the United States by greater incorporation of the expertise of the laity. Cardinal Roger Mahoney of Los Angeles has redirected much of the Church's political efforts into protecting the lives of immigrants to our country, reviving the Church's reputation for a commitment to outcasts with meaning, and bravely taking on rage at foreigners at a highly volatile and politically sensitive moment in the political life of the country. Groups like Voice of the Faithful, formed in Boston in the wake of the pedophile scandals, seek to hold the Church accountable for its actions. Catholics for a Free Choice advances teachings and thinking that advocate women's moral agency.

Instead of fleeing the Church as many have, we need to model ourselves as agents of change and use our power as the people of this Church to create improvements where they're needed and to laud and protect the many things that are valuable about our Church.

The Church is at its best when it joins its voice with people who are demanding their voices be heard. In Kenya, Liberia, Poland, Northern Ireland, South Korea, the Philippines, East Timor, Latin America, and so many other places over the past thirty years, I've been fortunate enough to witness the tremendous lifesaving aid, healing power, and pursuit of justice that is the work of the Catholic Church. In one country after another the Church is on the front lines of the struggle for human rights. I was never more proud to be a Catholic, as when I visited the Archdiocese of Monrovia. Liberia had endured fourteen years of civil war. In a country where a mere 7 percent of the population was Catholic, the Church never shuttered its schools, hospitals, clinics, and press even after the government and other religious missions had long since closed their doors.

While in Liberia, I spent one morning at the federal prison. Dante could've learned a lot from that place. A heavy stew of mold, waste, rot, urine, sweat, and tuberculosis was mixed with 100 percent humidity and cooked in hundred-degree F heat. The overcrowding, the starvation, the refuse in a common bucket in the corner of an eight-by-ten-foot dungeon were exacerbated by only enough ventilation for mosquitoes to fester. The lack of lawyers, visitors, blankets, electricity, or light gave one the sense of being a rat at the height of summer in a city sewer system. Family members rarely were able to visit, but the archdiocese never missed the weekly appointments, bringing food, medicines, and hope.

At one slum clinic I met a sister who dispensed medicine by candlelight, as it was too costly to run the generator for more than a few hours twice a week. In an HIV hospice, the Church ran out of antiretroviral medications three months earlier, but the sisters from the Missionaries of Charity were taking in new patients every day.

Again and again I was impressed by the deep commitment of so many Catholic leaders—highly educated women and men who easily could have landed far more lucrative and less dangerous positions overseas. Instead they stayed and, with hearts of fire, worked tirelessly on behalf of their country. It was impossible not to be moved by their love and grace.

At a camp for former child soldiers, I saw Samuel Kofi Woods restoring some sense of childhood to young teens who'd been forced to rape and murder loved ones.

Kofi knew brutality firsthand. As the founder of the Catholic radio station, his had been the voice of opposition to the brutal Charles Taylor dictatorship. He was imprisoned, tortured, and left to rot.

When a new democratic government came to power, Kofi's tormentors were tried for crimes against humanity. But they were so hated, no lawyer would take their case. For the sake of creating a reliable system of justice for Liberia, Kofi Woods, a true patriot, withstood the disdain of his countrymen and became defense counsel to his former torturers.

It is hard to imagine a greater example of Christlike love, forgiveness, faith, and service than that displayed by Samuel Kofi Woods. To those who suffer much, God grants uncommon wisdom.

Throughout the last quarter century, I've had the honor to work with courageous Catholics who've risked their lives and endured imprisonment, torture, and death for basic rights: free expression, freedom from torture, freedom of worship. They build civil societies; assure voting rights, free expression, and women's rights; and stop child labor, female genital mutilation, and honor killings. I've been deeply inspired by their commitment and capacity to create change against overwhelming odds. I feel proudest of my Catholicism when engaged with and witnessing the commitment of those who work on the front lines for social justice, as I've seen in the poorest and most violent places across the world. These are the people who seem closest to living out the faith of Jesus in word and deed.

My approach to social justice is captured in Catholic social teaching, a series of principles laid out by the Vatican and the U.S. Conference of Bishops, which outline the role of the Church and of Catholics in political and economic life. The doctrine embraces the inherent dignity of the person, the right and responsibility of each one of us to build community and work for the common good. It asserts that the moral test of a society is how it treats its most vulnerable members and demands that we look at public policy decisions in terms of how they affect the poor. It calls for the protection of human rights, including both political and economic rights. It insists that people have a right and a duty to participate in the political process. It recognizes economic justice, the right to a living wage, the right to form unions. It demands that we protect the environment, promote peace, work for disarmament, and pursue global justice.

The guidelines have come to define, for me, the essence of Catholicism in action. To the extent that the Church itself acts consistently with these principles, I feel at home and comfortable with the hierarchy. I find depth in the rich heritage of faith passed down to me through generations. I'm able to gain a sense of spirituality through prayer, service, and participation in the larger community. And I've come to realize that Catholicism is far more important than the pope and the bishops, our statues and icons, the confessional, the rosary beads, the smell of wax candles and incense, and our fabulous pageantry. Rather, Catholicism, in the end, is about creating a society based on a shared vision of God as exemplified by Christ, his commitment to justice and peace, and, most of all, his love.

For me, the last two years have been transformative. In this journey to make peace with the faith of my childhood and the tenets I want to teach my daughters, I've come to understand that we truly are a universal church, and at a billion strong there is a multitude of ways that people can live out their faith. I've witnessed the awesome power of prayer, I've experienced personally a renewed awakening of the peace and grace of simple faith, and I've felt a closeness to the Almighty that I haven't known since earliest childhood. I've been thinking about faith more than ever before, talking about it, reading about it, and, most important, working on it. I've attended morning prayer services at my parish, and I'm teaching the Confraternity of Christian Doctrine, or CCD (once known as Sunday school). I've started praying the Rosary and thinking of a reason to be grateful with every bead. Inevitably, I end this spiritual exercise feeling happy, uplifted, cheerful, and no surprise, grateful. It works! I went on a silent retreat with a wise Jesuit, one of the most healing and moving experiences of my life. And I've started to try, though I too often fail, to stop asking God for the outcome I desire and to ask instead for him to grant me the grace to be open to use my gifts so *his will be done.*

Sure, I'm irritated, frustrated, and enraged by some of the actions of the Church, but that's a sidebar to my sense of spirituality and of belonging to the Catholic faith. In the final analysis, the hierarchy of the Catholic Church isn't the end-all to my practice of the faith. From a political perspective, I wish it would become more active on peace and social justice because the pope and the bishops have enormous underutilized capacity to literally bring freedom to captives and, as Jesus did, invite more and more people to share his message of love. When I become incensed by the latest outrageous pronouncement of a wayward bishop, I try to remember that perhaps at this moment in history the Holy Spirit is sending lay Catholics an empowerment message that we can no longer be passive in our faith and blindly follow the hierarchy; instead, we must take personally the responsibility to act on the word of Christ despite the impediments placed in our path.

When I walk into church, dip my fingers in holy water, smell the candles, see the altar, kneel at the back of a pew, gaze up at Christ on the cross, and envelop myself in the stillness and blissful silence, I feel peaceful. When I'm at Mass, saying the Lord's Prayer aloud with the community of believers, I feel closer to God. When I sing along with everyone gathered together for the purpose of praising the Almighty, "They will know we are Christians by our love," I am deeply grateful to share in a faith that centers on love. When the priest holds the Eucharist and recalls the words of Jesus during his last supper on earth, I am in awe of Christ's courage and generosity. Then I think of the human rights defenders around the world who so love justice and humanity that, like Christ, they too have willingly sacrificed their lives for the sake of others.

When I think of my friends, my family, my wonderful daughters, and discern the common denominator of love and dignity in each, I'm grateful to God for endowing us each with special gifts, and the presence of the Holy Spirit in every human being. When we say prayers at night, and Cara, age thirteen, prays for those who help others, Michaela, age eleven, prays for the terrorists "because we need to love our enemies," and Mariah, age thirteen, adds "Dear God, I hope you have a great day because you really deserve it," I'm grateful for the call to service, the wisdom and the joy of our faith. When I think of my mother, Ethel; my grandmother Rose; my great-grandmother Mary Hannon; and my great-great-grandmother Bridget Murphy—when I consider the crosses they bore and how this faith sustained generations of women and men for two thousand years— I feel connected to the people who sacrificed so much and feel bonded to them through our common belief. I hope I'm able to pass on to my daughters the faith in the Almighty, the supremacy of love, the gift of hope, the enriching experience of being part of a faith community, and all the other positive aspects of our universal church—and yes, our rich heritage of a healthy sense of skepticism. And when I think of the beatitudes, I'm happy to be included in this wonderfully inclusive and affirming Catholic faith.

> *Blessed are the poor in spirit, for theirs is the kingdom of heaven.*
> *Blessed are they who mourn, for they will be comforted.*
> *Blessed are the meek, for they will inherit the earth.*

Blessed are they who hunger and thirst for righteousness, for they will be satisfied.

Blessed are the merciful, for they will be shown mercy.

Blessed are the clean of heart, for they will see God.

Blessed are the peacemakers, for they will be called children of God.

Blessed are they who are persecuted for the sake of righteousness, for theirs is the kingdom of heaven.

Blessed are you when they insult you and persecute you and utter every kind of evil against you falsely because of me.

Rejoice and be glad, for your reward will be great in heaven. Thus they persecuted the prophets who were before you.

(Matthew 5:3–10)

—KERRY KENNEDY
May 2008

BEING CATHOLIC NOW

ANNA QUINDLEN

Anna Quindlen (b. July 8, 1952) is a bestselling author and Pulitzer Prize—winning columnist. She joined the staff of Newsweek *in 1999, where she writes the* Last Word *column every other week.*

. . . .

When I was a kid, there were endless arguments that seemed to have no point. Whether it was proper, for example, if my parents went to a wedding in a Methodist church. This always seemed like the "How many angels can dance on a pin?" argument, since we were never invited to weddings that weren't in Catholic churches. In my entire neighborhood where I grew up there was no one who wasn't Catholic. No one had married into a family who wasn't Catholic.

There was a rhythm to the liturgical year, which gave this incredible shape to your life, in a way that had almost nothing to do with faith. It's like the distinction between the Baltimore Catechism and theology. The Baltimore Catechism gave this knee-jerk shape to every element of Catholicism that was absolutely anti-intellectual and unquestioning, as opposed to real theology. And so much of our lives as young Catholics was about that sort of ruling affirmative: What would happen if you unwittingly took a bite of a bologna sandwich on a Friday? Much of it was the functional equivalent of keeping kosher. Why does one do this? You don't ask this question, you just do it, unthinkingly, and there is supposed to be a virtue in the unthinking aspect of it, which of course was bound to catch up with me, sooner or later.

Real faith is something that happens later on.

It is the dichotomy that is in the Church today, which is that as an instrument of social justice, nobody does it better; but this is always overshadowed by the "shalt not" pronouncements that seem to have little to do with social justice, human frailty, or real faith. The Church is always in this state of huge dichotomy, when you look back through history, between form and function, between humanity and this rigid hierarchical rule making.

I'm struck by the fact that about 80 percent of what I care about politically is also what the Church supports. When I wrote a column in support of both legal and undocumented immigrants, I got a number of e-mail messages of support from priests, which was a first for me in recent years. And there is the zone of gynecological theology, where the Church is totally wrong. For American Catholics, the Church's stand on birth control or even abortion is, at some level, irrelevant. I'm talking about third-world Catholic women who, when they get pregnant, don't have an additional child but either die or have a baby who dies. The deep dichotomies of the Church are frustrating to me, especially because it does do so much good.

When our oldest child first described himself as an atheist, he was sixteen, and my husband and I looked at each other and said, "Right on schedule!" Until they went to college, our children had to go to Mass every Sunday. People would say to me, "Don't they get upset about that, not wanting to go?" But that is part of the tradition. We were part of that tradition too; we remember all the days when we said, "I don't want to go to Mass," and the response was "Get in the car."

Afterward, we would talk in the car about the sermon or the Gospel. Every year on Easter Sunday I'd start, and I could see the kids' eyes rolling, and I'd say, "Now notice, what is the first word Jesus said?" And from the backseat I would hear, "Woman." And I would go, "That is correct! He turns to Mary Magdalene and says, 'Woman, why are you crying?'" And by the fifth year it was like, "No Mom, not this thing about Mary Magdalene again."

They're clearly in the stage of their lives where their attitude is, if an institution doesn't work for you on a profound level, you don't need the institution. That may play out for the rest of their lives, because there's no question that they didn't have the Catholic upbringing I had. They didn't go to Catholic school; they weren't steeped in the "shalt not"s. I remember it controlling every aspect of my life.

I see them going through the process that we went through, when my husband, who's also a lifelong Catholic, and I were in college.

Both of us had very little, if anything, to do with the Church. Then we got married in the Church, and as soon we had kids, boom! We were right back where we started from, because there was no question that we were going to raise them Catholic, if only to give that kind of grounding from which to question, reject, move away, and maybe move back again.

As a kid, I had the classic models of heaven and hell—one is up, the other's down; one is cool, the other is hot; one is blue, the other is red.

My mother died when I was nineteen and then I thought about it all the time, about this notion of whether there was afterlife and if there was what it meant—whether the death of good people left a different vapor trail than the death of not so good people.

My own profound sense is that the most beloved people we know don't die; they're as real in our minds as they were when they could walk through the door. I'm more questioning and agnostic about that than I was when I was much younger, which is unfortunate, because now more than ever I need it to be true. I think that is the crux of a faith.

My greatest moral education came not from Catholic school or the Ten Commandments, but from my mother. It had more to do with being kind and generous in your dealings with other people. It had a lot more to do with empathy and humanity and less to do with the doctrinal approach. My mother had very strong feelings about right and wrong based on the New Testament approach of loving thy neighbor as thyself.

Many people seem to find this weird disconnect between my Catholic background and my political liberalism. The New Testament was such a profoundly politically liberal document that it is inconceivable to me that conservatism has come out of it. It's driven explicitly and constantly by this need to do better by other people, by this moral obligation to do your best by and for others. That shaped my political sense in every way.

If you understand history, you understand the extent to which

Jesus hung around with unrelated women. It's so outside the realm of proper behavior; he had to have been trying to teach us something by that.

I don't do Catholic guilt. I don't feel guilty about being at odds with the Church over the things I'm at odds with them over.

As a child, I internalized the sense that I didn't need to feel that bad about anything, because I could make it better on a Saturday afternoon in a dark place. When we first started to go to confession, we really had nothing to confess; that is why we made everything up. And by the time we really had things to confess, either they were things that the Church had taught us were so shameful that we didn't want to confess them, or they seemed too amorphous to be confessable.

If I were pope for a year, I'd be the second woman pope. The first thing I would do is ordain women because that would lift the Church. In many ways we have seen society change for the better with women at high levels—in business, in the judiciary, and in politics. What we would see in the Church is a completely different approach to attitudes across the board; we would revive parishes throughout this country and the world. There are many women waiting in the wings. Then I would bring those women priests together for a special synod with their male counterparts.

Part of the problem with the Church is that it knows how to talk but doesn't know how to listen. I would probably spend six months with people just listening to one another. Then I would lift the ban on artificial birth control, especially in third-world countries, and say that people should keep themselves safe through condom use. In vitro fertilization—that's absolutely an absurd prohibition. I'd promote a humane approach to death; I was very sad when the Church involved itself in the Terri Schiavo case in inappropriate ways.

I'd also look for a more conciliatory, humane Christlike attitude toward Catholics who have divorced. The Church has caused so much pain and so much cynicism about the annulment process, which has become the Church exercising control over the divorce process and has nothing to do with what we used to think of as annulment. All of my sister priests would be doing the same thing, so I'd be in really good company.

John Paul epitomized the dichotomy I was talking about, and the dovetailing of his papacy and the sex abuse scandals were very hard on my relationship with the Institutional Church. For a while, I went a little in and a little out in terms of going to Mass every Sunday. The parish in which we worship helped my perspective of the Institutional Church, because it's run by the Paulist fathers. It's a church that does everything that a good church should do, from engaging parishioners in the actual form of the Mass to providing all kinds of social services that are so important in its neighborhood. But I've been struggling with my relationship with the Institutional Church and whether I ratify what I consider the negative things it does in its name by attending Mass.

On the other hand, I feel proud of being a Catholic in fits and starts all the time. As a reporter, I was so proud of being Catholic so much of the time, because I had this sort of constant experience where someone would say, I know that you are really interested in teenage pregnancy and there is this great program for teen mothers. So I would go, and the person who was running the program would take me around and talk about what she was doing and how many young women were there and so on. I would be looking around for twenty minutes and then look at her and look at the pantsuit, look at the shoes, and ask her, "Are you a nun?" "Yes," she'd say, but she wouldn't want me to call her "Sister."

I get e-mails all the time when I touch on anything Catholic. People say, "I know your kind; you memorized the Baltimore Catechism, but you don't go to Mass, you're divorced, and you've had an abortion." And I think if these people could only see me every Sunday morning, if these people only knew that I was married in the Church, that all of my children have lived through the sacraments. People presume these things when you're politically liberal, and yet some of the most thoughtful and intelligent liberals I know are practicing Catholics.

On the other hand, there is a substantial group of intelligent and thoughtful people who are incredulous that you could have anything still to do with the Church as a person of thought and intellect. It is an acceptable bias to assume that at some level Catholicism is just dumb.

ANDREW SULLIVAN

Andrew Sullivan (b. August 10, 1963) is one of today's most provocative social and political commentators. Senior editor at the Atlantic, *and a columnist for the* Sunday Times *of London, he is also the editor of the* Daily Dish, *one of the most widely read political blogs on the Web.*

Sullivan is known for his unusual personal-political identity. He is HIV-positive, gay, libertarian, a conservative often at odds with other conservatives, and a practicing Catholic.

. . . .

I grew up in a small town in the English countryside and was always outside. My mother threw us out every morning, as long as we were back by the time it got dark. It was a different world, and I always accepted that the beauty of the countryside that I lived in was a mark of something that I couldn't explain. It was more than what it appeared to be. Every May, in my little church, we would bring in the blossoms for the Month of Our Lady and that celebration of unity of nature with God was something that I grew up breathing. I didn't have a fire-and-brimstone Catholic upbringing. I had a slightly hippie-dippy, lovey-dovey, post–Vatican II Catholic upbringing.

Both my parents were born in England, but our lineage was from western Ireland. We grew up as Catholics in a Protestant country, and I always felt marginalized to some extent through my faith, which absolutely strengthened it. You'd better defend your identity.

I went to a Catholic primary school until age ten. I was supposed to go to Catholic secondary school, but the only school that would accept me was horrifying to my parents. I went to the Protestant school, which was a big deal for our family. My grandmother was terribly upset, but for my faith, it was the best thing they could've done for me. I might have rebelled against an austere Catholic secondary school. From the beginning, I felt I had to defend myself against these Protestants. And when you're fighting that fight, you assume the existence of God in the first place. So it sunk in.

Growing up in England in the 1960s and 1970s was pretty awful, depressing, tawdry, and church for me, just walking in there, was something beyond all of this. There was something dark, mysterious, and beautiful beyond all these supermarkets, McDonald's, bad television, and strikes. You walk in as an altar boy and smell the different smell, feel the different air, and see the light refracted through different windows. It tells you, this is not the rest of the world. There's a line from Larkin in my head: "A serious house on serious earth this is." I got a very severe and clear signal that *this matters.* Don't you mess with this, don't you belittle this. We weren't corralled or anything, but my family was very insistent that we take this seriously. I wanted to figure it all out.

My confirmation saint was Thomas More. He was an absolute authoritarian in the Church and I think, in retrospect, did some things that I find abhorrent. He was happy to send people to the stake. On the other hand, he also clearly placed his conscience at the center of his life. If he was asked to do something, by all of the authorities that he lived up to—by the law of the land, by the very king whom he served—he'd still say no if his conscience said otherwise. He was both an authoritarian and a real rebel. He captured what it means to be Catholic. So when I came to be confirmed, I picked him.

As a teenager, my Catholic identity was very important to me. It still is. People always ask me, in the last ten years especially, why don't you just become an Episcopalian? My answer is: I would if I could. I don't really have a choice in this matter. I'd sooner become a Muslim. The ferocity of my upbringing and the nature of that conflict would mean embracing something that I'd defined myself against for thirty years. I've come to realize that my disdain for Protestantism was exaggerated, that I slipped into many of the fundamentalist traps that I've subsequently understood to be traps. Nevertheless, I'm a human being. We can't be remade overnight. I have nowhere else to go. This is absolutely my home. It's the only place I feel comfortable.

Look at the polling. You'll find Catholics supporting the positions the Episcopalian Church already accepts, but that is not what my faith is about. We're asked, first of all, to believe that God exists, which, compared to what our position is on stem cell research, seems to me to be a much more fundamental issue. Second, we're asked to believe that God is love, which to my mind is a much bigger step. So if I'm prepared to believe all that, and in fact I find myself unable not to believe that, why would I leave on a trivial issue like whether women should be priests or not? Faith isn't like picking courses off a menu. It's a journey, and it's a path. If your path and journey have been within one structure your entire life, then simply leaving isn't an option.

I used to always go to St. Matthew's Cathedral in Washington, D.C. Cardinal McCarrick was a breath of fresh air. He's such an obviously Christian person. During the 2004 presidential election, McCarrick did something that didn't get much publicity. At the time, Cardinal Ratzinger (now Pope Benedict) was head of the Congregation for the Propagation of the Doctrine of the Faith. There was a meeting that the bishops convened to determine whether John Kerry or other leading Catholic politicians would be officially banned from receiving Communion, and McCarrick was quite adamant in resisting any blanket policy. And he won the day, thank God.

But it was much closer than people realize, and in fact, Ratzinger had sent McCarrick a letter in which he essentially said, "Go ahead. Take the public stance saying that anybody who doesn't have the exact position on abortion that we do will not be eligible for Communion." McCarrick withheld the letter. That's what I am told. He just did not want to press the thing, because that would have led to a genuine crisis. The Catholic bishops in this country, at least a plurality of them, would have said no, and there would have been a huge fight with Rome. In the middle of an election, I think McCarrick's prudential decision was that it would have hurt the Church more than it would have helped. He had already been told, but he ignored it. He buried it.

It does matter when I disagree with the pope. I've been trying to out-argue the hierarchy for twenty years on one particular subject. Their whole doctrine of sexuality is so fraught with internal contradiction. It's your job to ask yourself, what are they asking me to believe? I studied quite intensely the theological arguments about the impermissibility of anything except procreative marital heterosexual sex and thought them through. I engaged the hierarchy at a rational level and came to the conclusion that they didn't actually make sense, on their own terms, nor did they really speak truthfully to either the biological evidence and knowledge that we currently have about what human beings are or to my own experience of what the phenomenon of homosexual orientation is. My obligation, therefore, as a Catholic, is to bring this forward and say, tell me where I'm wrong. The truth matters.

By and large, I've never experienced any hostility from my fellow Catholics as a gay man. When I walk into the church, I'm one soul. I'm no more, no less, than anyone else there. My politics, my gender, my orientation—anything else I leave behind seems to me to be left behind. The genius of Paul's Christianity is that we leave all that behind. It's an amazing liberation.

I'm able to say to myself as a gay man (and maybe this is an incredible cheat on my part): I just know the Church isn't right. I let it go. Catholics throughout the last two millennia have lived in the Church when it is doing things they don't agree with. They either go insane or they let it go, work from within, or concentrate on what matters, which is the Gospel of Jesus, the sacraments that incarnate the message of Jesus, and the personhood of Jesus. They try to live their lives as they should, as we're asked to live. The Gospel of Jesus is constantly saying don't lose sight—that's really all that matters. All these laws, let them all go, if you love. If you have them all but you don't love, it means nothing.

When I look around me at all the priests, I know so many of them are gay. You're demonized to the very core of who you are—the very impulse to love another person. It's not like you're demonized because you're not smart enough. It's love at its core that is being attacked, your emotional identity and dignity as a person. They're basically telling me I'm sick, that I can't be cured, and that I'm to live my life alone, forever. It's deeply psychologically damaging, and I think a lot of my own issues as an adult with sex and love are connected to that damage. I've been in therapy for a long time.

Someone once asked me, "Do you think the Church will change its mind?" Not in my lifetime. I came to a point where I don't need them to relinquish. I wish they would. But I'm reconciled to that. As Catholics, we're taught not to judge our positions on their success but rather on whether they're true or not. All you can do is ask yourself, deep in your soul, "Am I genuinely right on this?"

The staggering moment for me in the Gospels is the moment, on the cross, when Jesus is about to die. He openly doubts whether he's not been mistaken about all of it. "My God, my God, why have you forsaken me?" He's questioning God; he's questioning all of it. And this is *Jesus* on the cross, at the moment of his greatest triumph; almost his last words are: Did I get all of this wrong? Am I really alone?

If you were creating a legend of a great hero who died, you wouldn't interpolate a moment of weakness at the end. I think it's real. I think it happened. And it's very human. So, doubt and fear and imperfection are at the core of our faith. One shouldn't be afraid of doubt as long as it's part of a process in which you're trying to figure out what's true. The only person who can ever answer that is you, alone with God.

The Martha and Mary Gospel passage is the one that's always been with me and really kept me sane during my own experience of HIV. I was basically told, you're going to die, and my best friend and my boyfriend were told at the same time. It was a very grim time. And the day after I found out, I found myself drawn to that passage again.

It's a very simple story. Jesus shows up unannounced and Mary and Martha have these two opposite responses to his coming. Martha does what really we all should do, make sure that dinner is fixed and everything is okay, and Mary just sits at Jesus' feet and listens. Jesus has this beautiful sentence, which is, first of all, "Martha, Martha"—he repeats her name twice, which is a sign of intimacy—"you fret and are anxious about so many things but only one thing matters. Mary has chosen the better part. Don't take it away from her." He's not even judging Martha; he's sympathizing with her and her perplexity, her distraction, her anxiety, and he isn't even telling her not to do what she's doing. He's just saying, "Look, Mary's here and she's with me, and that's all that really matters."

When you think about it from the context of history, here's the son of God walking into your house, and you go to the kitchen? Why are you missing a second of the presence of Jesus? How many people in human history have that opportunity? Then there's this question: What does he mean that only one thing is necessary? This is a big thing for Jesus to say. What was the coded message of this? I think it's hiding in plain sight, meaning simply Mary is being with me, which is being here for each other now. I love her, she loves me, and we're spending time together. The message of the incarnation is that God is with us. I think we've become so used to the idea that God is with us that we don't realize how revolutionary an idea that is.

I don't know if there's a heaven and hell. When my friend Patrick was dying, we had this conversation: He said to me, "I'm scared," and I said to him, "What are you scared of?" He said, "I'm scared that there'll be nothing." There's nothing to say to that when someone literally is confronting their death. He was thirty years old. All I did was hold him. That's all I could do. I had no answer. I'm absolutely convinced that I felt Patrick's spiritual presence after his death *very* powerfully. I believe that Patrick didn't die.

Everybody seems to have a different analysis of what it meant for Jesus to be resurrected. Some of them see him in the vision of another person. Then there are moments when he seems to just disappear completely. There's not a scientific explanation of what this resurrection means except to say that his disciples clearly experienced his existence after death in as vivid a way as they experienced him in life.

In a much more trivial way, I think, because obviously Patrick wasn't Jesus, I felt him around; I *still* feel him around, and I pray to him and think of him. In that sense, these are mysteries that I don't know. I don't believe it's the end, but I don't know fully and could not articulate what it can and will mean. I think it means some sort of unity with God's love, but I certainly don't believe in some sort of reward system. I don't believe in anybody who claims to know. I'm convinced death is not the end.

The fundamental values that I was taught were twofold: to love one's neighbor and to tell the truth. Those were two very, very clear injunctions. I've been better with the latter rather than the former! So, for example, when people would ask me occasionally, "How can you be openly gay and Catholic?" my response has been I'm openly gay *because* I'm Catholic, because I was taught not to lie and because I was taught to have nothing to fear, from my Church, from the truth, or from God.

I've long believed that Jesus had no politics, that there were no politics in the Gospels. It's quite remarkable how Jesus avoids politics even when he's in a very political system and a very political moment with extreme political pressures. He's almost fanatically devoted to not taking a position because he's obsessed with telling people, "That's the wrong question." The question is this: How are you living now? Not how the system could be reformed. Not how the world could be made a better place. *You* serving the poor—it doesn't talk about *service* to the poor as an abstract construct. He says, "Give everything to the poor."

How one constructs a political order will depend upon different questions about what's practicable in a fallen world to minimize the harm we do to one another.

Jesus' call to us is to serve one another now. He cites various situations in which we're supposed to help: the homeless, the imprisoned, the sick, and the poor. Your obligation as a human being, as a follower of Jesus, is to alleviate that suffering immediately. And, again, we can't live up to this. We don't. We walk past it every day. But I don't think that within Christianity there is an argument that the government should be redistributing wealth from one group of people to another or that the government has a responsibility to do this, that, or another. I can see how people can infer that, but that step is a problematic one. We can construct politics entirely on realistic grounds, on the basis of wicked human nature, and then keep this government as limited as possible, and then Jesus' message is for you to transform yourself, not anybody else.

There is a great documentary called *Saint of 9/11* about Father Mychal Judge. He was the firefighters' chaplain who died at the World Trade Center.

This is a man who never had a checking account, who spent his life walking the streets. You'll see the face of Jesus in everything he did. There's one story that had me in tears, because it reaches the heart. When AIDS first hit New York City, the first people started showing up at St. Vincent's with this strange illness and they were all gay. Judge himself was gay but very much on the down low. His impulse as a Franciscan was to go there, to be with the sick. And as he walked up to one of their hospital rooms, he said their first impulse upon seeing a man of the Church was flinching away because they felt, oh God, these people are coming to judge me, and they wouldn't let him in the room.

When they fell asleep, he went into their rooms, lifted the bottom of the sheet up to expose their feet, and he put oil on them. They would wake up and see him doing what Jesus did. And the cycle was broken. This service—it was a beautiful moment of Christian love. He won them back slowly.

These people were going insane. They didn't know why they had lesions. They started losing weight and couldn't absorb anything. They had no drugs to deal with any of these sudden new illnesses, which they'd never seen before because the immune system had always beaten them back. And to be able to come into that situation, defuse it, and give them composure, calm, peace, and love— that makes me proud to be Catholic.

BILL O'REILLY

ED BERNIK

Bill O'Reilly (b. September 10, 1949) is an author, syndicated columnist, and American political commentator on television and talk radio. He is the host of The O'Reilly Factor *on* FOX News Channel, *the most-watched program on cable news.*

. . . .

My parents were both Irish and their tradition was to go to church every Sunday. I went to Catholic schools and Marist College. It was traditional—no meat on Friday, just straight down the Irish Catholic line.

My mother was religious. My father was more casual, but they did go to church and they were respectful. Priests came over once in a while for dinner. It was built into the fabric of the tradition of the O'Reillys and Kennedys. My mother's a Kennedy on her mother's side.

It was just accepted that in my neighborhood most people were Catholic or Jewish. It was Italian, Polish, Irish, or Jewish. I don't think I knew any Protestants. I enjoyed being an altar boy. I'd get tipped if I did funerals or weddings. I didn't want to, because you have to learn all the Latin prayers and who wants to do that when you're ten? My mother forced me. But once I got in there, I figured I could make some money.

I thought about becoming a priest for maybe ten minutes, but that really wasn't my career path. I wasn't a devout kid. The nuns would constantly tell me that I was going to hell, and I'd say, "Okay, my friends will be there, so it'll be fun."

I don't think it's important that you understand the concept of heaven. It can't be defined. I believe that there is a struggle between good and evil in this world. You choose whether to be good, bad, or apathetic. Then the struggle between good and evil plays out in various ways and the good people, when they die, will be rewarded and the bad people will be punished.

Everyone I've ever met, even the severely mentally deficient people, all have talent somewhere. And if there weren't a God, that wouldn't happen. That's one reason I believe in God. The other reason is that nature is never a miscommunication: Sun goes up, sun goes down; tide comes in, tide goes out; seasons come, and seasons go. But everything that man is involved in gets fouled up one way or another on some level. Nature doesn't get fouled up. Storm comes, regeneration. So when you look at the overall picture, I say no meteorite could possibly have crashed and caused nature to be so perfect. There had to be a more sophisticated presence to make that happen, so that's the genesis of my faith.

The nuns to me were amusing. It was always a cat-and-mouse game between O'Reilly and Sister Mary Carol—whether I was going to get away with whatever con I was running that day. I never took the nuns as seriously as some of my classmates did.

I've always gone to church, even in the Woodstock era when I was the only one in the chapel and the old priest and I were looking at each other. The reason is that the tradition of the Roman Catholic Church is helpful to me. I like the structure. I like the fact that an hour a week I'm in this environment that I'm not in at any other time. I'm not judgmental. I don't proselytize. Because television is the most secular business in the world, I'm probably one of the very few people in the building who goes to church every week. It was always about what was helpful to me as a person rather than what the nuns told me or being afraid to go to hell. I've always had that outsider view. You can see it on television, in journalism, in my writing, where I look at things outside, not inside, and try to formulate the best plan to accomplish what I want.

I believe that the inherent gifts I was born with should be used in a positive way. I was born with a writing ability, the ability to speak, and I'm presentable looking. So I packaged that into a television career. Then I decided, once I was fairly successful in television, to try to use it to advance causes that protect children and hold scoundrels accountable for their bad deeds.

I made a decision to use my skill and my position to be an advocate for certain things. I understood when I got into that arena that the *New York Times*—and the people who disagree with me—would try to hurt me. I didn't take it seriously enough in the beginning. Now I do. The danger involved bleeds over to my family, which is really the reason that Jesus never got married and the reason the Church doesn't want priests to get married. I'm well paid to take it, but it's the worst part of this whole battle between secularism and traditionalism.

I don't go at it from a "protecting Catholicism" point of view; it's protecting the culture. It's quite clear to any honest person reading about the formation of the country that the founding fathers had no problem with the cross or any other public display of religion. The Ten Commandments are in the Supreme Court. The secular progressives understand that what stands between them and their vision of secular nirvana are religious people who make judgments about abortion, gay marriage, euthanasia, legalized narcotics, war and peace, all the way down the line.

That's what the Christmas battle is all about: Get it out. De-emphasize all religion and spirituality in the marketplace. Then you'll have children who have no frame of reference at all who will be easily persuaded to go the secular route. If you're offended by the manger scene, then you're nuts. It's a baby in a stable surrounded by his loving parents. We're not set up to give in to somebody's nutty neurosis. Before I got involved with the Christmas battle, the secular progressives were winning. They had big corporations ordering employees not to say "Merry Christmas" and banishing Christmas from the storefronts. We turned the assault on Christmas around fast. The Christmas battle's won now, but it'll come back again.

I've been to seventy-two countries, covered four wars, and I know there's good, there's evil, and there's a battle. Do most people who are evil realize that they're evil? No, they're too narcissistic. I confronted a Nazi concentration guard in Dachau and said, "How could you?" He said, "I was ordered to." Ordered? He had a gun. He has two feet. They all have excuses.

I don't have any Catholic guilt. In eighth grade we were told that French kissing was the road to hell. You figure out, wait a minute, there are people getting murdered in the street, stealing stuff, and beating up others, and I'm going to be down there with them if I kiss Sally? It never calibrated with me, but I do make a conscious effort to realize when I do bad things and to correct those bad things.

The whole Catholic faith is based on forgiveness and reconciliation. If somebody asks me to forgive them, I instantly do.

Before I go after somebody, and I do go after people, I warn them. When John Edwards had those two anti-Catholic bloggers on staff saying those horrible things, I called him four times. I said, we don't want to do this story, but you have got to get rid of them. He basically said, "F-you." That wasn't about Catholicism. That was about somebody who wants to be president of the United States employing two haters and having no reason why. He would've never employed them if those people had been anti-Semitic or even anti-Muslim. So why should I allow that to happen without comment?

I've been reading the Bible more now that I'm an old guy. There are a lot of very interesting things when you read it slowly, for knowledge rather than to find a passage to throw at somebody you want to demean. Religion shouldn't be used in that way—as a club. That's happened to a lot of the secularists and atheists that I know, and people who have fallen away from the faith; they resent the fact that religion has been used to brutalize them in some way. Cardinal Law is a villain. I got him removed from office in Boston. I pounded him relentlessly, because he was not doing what he should have for the protection of children in this country. It wasn't a Catholic thing. It could have been a rabbi. I don't care who he is. Just because you've got a red cap doesn't give you a pass. He chose to do what he did. This is my job. I hope I'm not excommunicated. I try to be good, but I'm not a zombie.

I couldn't possibly be pope for a year. I'm the biggest sinner in the world, so the Vatican would have to close.

I think the Catholic Church in the modern era is making two major mistakes. Number one is not applying theology to America's relevant social issues. How many times do I need to hear about the mustard seed? I got it. It fell on fallow ground. But every year I've got to listen to the guy tell me about the mustard seed. My three-year-old's got it. OK, take it, apply it to what we're doing, how we're living. That's why only 25 percent of American Catholics show up every week. There's no relevancy. The Catholic Church's got to get out of the narrow-minded "This is our tradition" and apply the faith to the modern world. It does not do it on a general basis. So if I were in power as, let's say, an adviser to the Vatican, I would say, get your bishops, get a senate in here, and explain to them that the homily matters. It should be ten minutes long and it should deal with stuff that people have to deal with instead of this mustard seed business.

Number two is that the Church doesn't have leadership in the clergy. The cardinal of New York never comes out of his mansion. What's he doing? Go up to Harlem, tell people who you are, why you do what you do, and what you believe, instead of sitting up there in your mansion, doing jack and closing Catholic schools.

I stay a Catholic because I believe in the faith if you look at it from top to bottom. It's very pure. And if everyone lived the way that Jesus lived, we wouldn't have any problems on this earth. I have no problem with the fundamental tenets of the faith; it's the men who implement it that screwed it up. I respect some of them. I give a lot of money to them.

Catholic school is different than it was when I was there. The administration is enlightened. My kids go to Catholic school. I see the difference between the way my daughter and her friends behave as opposed to the public school kids. The crudities that are accepted in public school are enormous. I don't want that. I want my kids to be kids as long as they can be. I don't want them quoting rap lyrics. There's no brainwashing; my daughter doesn't memorize the catechism, but the teachers make it fun and interesting. She likes the rituals, she sings the songs, and she's happy. That's my primary goal, to protect her and make sure she's happy.

COKIE ROBERTS

Cokie Roberts (b. December 27, 1943) is a senior news analyst for NPR, where she was the congressional corre-spondent for more than ten years. She is also a political commentator for ABC News, serving as an on-air analyst for the network.

. . . .

I grew up in an intensely Catholic family where there was no question that you were Catholic. I went to very fine Catholic schools
run by the Religious of the Sacred Heart. It was the 1950s and these
women took girls seriously when nobody else did. I enjoyed the
schools greatly and as I got older came to appreciate them greatly. At
this point in my life, I consider them to be the most important influence other than my parents, husband, and children.

I grew up in a political family, which means there were advantages
and disadvantages of being Catholic, and that tends to concentrate
the mind. For instance, when my father was running for governor of
Louisiana, the election was in early 1952, but the race itself was in
1951. The fact that he was Catholic was a huge political problem.
Earl Long would go around northern Louisiana, which is all Baptist,
saying, "They're sayin' down there in *South* Louisiana"—which is
strike one against you—"that Hale Boggs is a Communist"—strike
two. "Now, we know that's not true; Hale Boggs is no Communist.
He can't be. He's a good Catholic boy." Much worse. "They say down
there in *South* Louisiana, well if Hale Boggs is elected, the pope of
Rome himself is going to come here and run Louisiana. Now you
know that's not true. The pope of Rome is a very busy man. But the
archbishop of New Orleans isn't." It was very much a situation where
you knew that being Catholic had its political risks and the effect of
that is it makes you more Catholic.

My family was always cosmopolitan, partly because of being in
politics. So I knew people from many faiths. In fact, the one thing
that I didn't know was ethnic prejudice. I certainly knew racial prejudice all too well, and I knew religious prejudice, but I was in college
before I knew there were people who had prejudice against Italians
or Irish or Jews.

It was an issue with the nuns when I went to Wellesley, a non-Catholic college. This was in a very brief period of time in American history when you had a large cadre of educated Catholics, but they were still insular. When people became more educated, they became less insular. But at that point it was still true, and, also, all of these religious orders had created their own colleges and had a vested interest in sending people to them.

At various points I wanted to become a nun. I think every little girl taught by nuns at some point does, because you admire these women so much. When you looked around at women in the 1950s, your role models were few and far between. And if you wanted to find somebody who was doing something really interesting and smart, it was likely to be a nun.

My husband, Steve, whom I met in college, is Jewish. When Steve and I started dating we were a little wary and it was much worse on his end than on mine. It was unusual in 1966 for a Catholic and a Jew to get married, but it's never been an issue in our marriage. Our families got over it fast, and my family was basically fine with it.

I believe my faith has impacted my marriage in very positive ways. We both admire the part of the person that we are because of our faiths. Steve says that very explicitly. It's not despite the fact that I'm a Catholic that he loves me; it's because of the fact that I'm a Catholic, and that came as something of a surprise to him. I think he feels that my Catholicism has informed my sense of generosity and caring in a way that he respects and admires. There's a strong sense of tradition and justice in the Jewish community, and particularly in Steve, which I feel attached to.

We raised our kids as both. How was the Church going to respond to it? How could it say no? There's no intersection. It's ridiculous that the Church would deny a Jewish godparent. The truth of it is, any one of us can baptize a child. It's just some priest deciding to pull some power game. This gets to the broader question, which is, why do you stay in this organization when people say stupid things like that? There are all kinds of reasons. But the only way you can deal with people like that is to just go around them. I just dismiss them; often they don't know what they're talking about, and if they pull out Canon Law 456, you can always pull out Canon Law 321. I mean, it's the most ambiguous institution on earth, *on purpose.* It hasn't been around for two thousand years by acting straightforward all the time.

Going into journalism in some ways—and in my case a lot of it— was just haphazard, because I was a woman of a certain age doing what I could do wherever I was at various times of my life. Trying to explain the workings of government, the situations of people who are not as well off or as equally treated, certainly comes out of that, so that the body politic understands what's going on. And, of course, I've always been involved in good causes, and at this point in my life that's a huge part of what I do.

I spoke this fall to Catholic Charities, which had just come out with this fabulously researched study on poverty in America, including this *phenomenal* statistic—that one in every two Americans will spend some portion of their adult lives in poverty. There were all these wonderful people in this room, who spend their lives all day, every day, working with the disadvantaged and the poor and the children and the pregnant women and everybody in society they can help. They said to me, "How do we get this message out?" I said, "Look, you've got Catholics trapped in churches every Sunday for hours on end. You know there are five masses. And the people who should be preaching about income discrepancy are the people who are in front of those Catholics every Sunday. You've got to do a lot better outreach on your own, with your own parishes and through the bishops."

About a month later, after this remarkable study comes out, the Catholic bishops meet—and what do they talk about? They talk about gay marriage and birth control. It's as if they're asking to have their authority completely ignored. *Birth control*—I mean, come on! An issue that has been decided by American Catholics. They did some little nod to the fact that we're at war, but they could've taken this report from their own social service agency and said, "Okay, this is our mission." The truth is, the bishops do that in the halls of Congress. They're lobbyists for health care, for welfare, and for all of those things. But the only thing anybody hears them on is abortion.

The part about girls not being altar servers—that's so absurd. As with all other things when they have become sexually integrated, people discover the only group that is responsible enough to show up, that you can count on, is women or, in this case, girls. So what's happening in church is that often there are only girls to serve because they're the ones who show up on time and do as they're supposed to do!

I always joke that in the Sacred Heart School, when you are about five years old, you learn about St. Philippine Duchesne, this remarkable woman who comes to this country in her forties, manages to get across the Atlantic, this dangerous crossing, and has been told by the bishop of St. Louis that he will help her in her quest to educate the Indians. It's a terrible voyage, and when she comes up the Mississippi and gets to St. Louis, the bishop says to her, "Never mind, I didn't mean it, and by the way, leave St. Louis; it's never going to amount to anything. St. Charles is going to be opening to the West." And my joke always is this: So as a five-year-old in Sacred Heart School you learn that the bishop has lied to the saint. She wasn't a saint in my year, but she is now. The bishop lied to her and he has it wrong; he is not very bright. Nothing happens to change that view.

And that gets to our essential question: Why stay Catholic? Because the hierarchy is not the Church. If the hierarchy were the Church, you would never have had a Church survive for two thousand years. Fortunately, in Vatican II, it was said pretty explicitly that the Church is the people of God. We're the Church. They can't take that away from us. The notion of leaving the Church would just be to give them a victory, and I'm not about to do that. They aren't winning.

I disagree with the Church all the time. There's hardly ever a time that I agree with it, except on social justice issues. And I'm a great believer in the culture of life. I do believe that there's a role for counterculturalism on the part of the Church, to stand up for marriage even though it gets all kind of crazy in the business of annulment. The Church should be a universal, respected institution that speaks for the poor; again, John Paul, for all of his doctrinal issues where you could get in a snip with him, was very clear on the preferential option for the poor. We miss hearing that in the pulpit. I only know the words "preferential option for the poor" because I've covered the Vatican, and nothing can be as off-putting as that.

You just do what works; you pay the hierarchy respect, and you do it all in a very gracious manner. But you go on and do what has to be done. When Pope Benedict was about to be elected, and I was in Rome for John Paul's funeral, I said to one of my aunts, who is ninety-two, and quite a devout Catholic, "I think this pope could be a problem." And she said, "Oh well." I used to tease my mother that she was the only person I knew who could move to the Vatican and come home Catholic. He doesn't matter to a lot of Catholics. The pope means something to the nuns. They're the people who feel completely disenfranchised and marginalized. But thank God for them. They're the voice of redemption.

I pray all the time. I actually say my prayers as I walk out to get the newspaper. It's a way of dealing with things. The breast cancer treatment that I take—the hormones—gives you terrible hot flashes, so when I have an uncomfortable flash, I offer it up for everybody with cancer and sometimes name names if somebody's in a particularly bad situation. What I mainly pray about is saying thank you for all the many blessings. Oh, sure, I talk to God. I don't think I hear much. That would be a little spooky!

As a Catholic, you don't spend much time reading the Bible! We said the Rosary all the time as kids, which drove my poor father crazy. I consider the letter of St. James the politician's letter. Basically, his message is, by your works, you shall know him. Enough with all this faith; let's see a few actions here. The Letter of St. James passage, verse 14, reads: "My brothers, what is the good of a man saying he has faith if he has no good deeds to show. Can faith save him? If some brother or sister has no clothes and has no food enough for a day and one of you says to them, good-bye, keep warm and have plenty to eat without giving them the necessaries of life, what good does it do? So faith by itself, if it has no good deeds to show, is dead."

Catholic guilt is all about sex. But that's not entirely true. A lot of it's about knowing that you're supposed to do the right thing, and if you don't do it you feel bad. Guilt is a good thing. It's the civilizing influence. My children feel a little bit burdened by the fact that they have both Catholic and Jewish guilt!

John Paul pretty much got rid of heaven as a place. It was actually a very solid intellectual thing. He was saying heaven is being in the presence of God; it's not some place up there with angels and stuff. Don't expect to *move*! I hope that's right. I hope that there is something after this where you are in some state where you feel complete and where you do check in with people you've missed—your family and friends.

I'm with Teilhard de Chardin on the subject of hell. Chardin says, I believe in hell because the theological virtue of faith makes me believe in hell, but the theological virtue of charity makes me exercise the theological virtue of hope that no one is there!

The first thing I would do if I were pope is ordain women and then married men. Let them see how easy it is to have wives. Every institution that we know of has been improved by the presence of women.

Catholicism is a place that gives me a solid sense of justice, hope, and love. If the message of the Church is "God is love," and he is going to nourish, going to love you no matter what you do, then that is the message that I believe. I think that message empowers everybody and makes everyone a better person.

I went to the pontifical Mass, which was quite beautiful because John Paul was so aware of television that he cleaned up St. Peter's and then put TV lights in so you could see the mosaics in ways you had never seen them before. But, of course, it was all of these men in vestments, and there were no women, anywhere, anywhere, anywhere. It was just very isolating to me. I felt very much not part of it, and I was feeling very blue.

It was a pretty night, it was fall, and I walked across the river and found myself just wandering. Ultimately, I came to the bottom of the Spanish Steps. So I walked up, and there was Trinita dei Monte, the mother house of the Sacred Heart order. I knocked on the door and since the order originated in France, I said in my horrible French, "Can I come see Mater?" And they said, "Sure, come on in." Then they said, "You know, we're doing a First Communion; would you like to come in the chapel?" I walked in the chapel and there were these children on the altar with puppets and nuns on the altar with puppets. There was this joy and this love and this complete acceptance of everyone being part of it. And I said, "*This* is my church." They can't run me out of this church no matter how hard they try. And that sense of inclusion that you feel when you are with other Catholics, and with people who have been raised in the same way, and have the same like-mindedness and sense of love and giving, is very strong.

There have been lots of times that I've been proud to be Catholic. Right now, Nancy Pelosi talking about her Catholic roots and having the Mass at Trinity College is a wonderful moment. When Geraldine Ferraro came back to Congress after she'd been nominated for vice president, she came onto the floor, and all the congress-women of both parties—there weren't that many—came and sat in the front rows and gave the one-minute speeches at the beginning of Congress, and a bunch of them stood up and said none of us would be here without the nuns.

My aunt, who never had any money, always had the slogan "If there's room in the heart, there's room in the home." With her own seven children, she would always take in more of us and never complain about it. All of that was out of the spirit of Catholicism.

BILL MAHER

Bill Maher (b. January 20, 1956) is an American comedian, actor, writer, and producer. He hosted the late-night television talk show Politically Incorrect *on Comedy Central and ABC and is currently the star of* Real Time with Bill Maher *on HBO. He also hosted* Amazon Fishbowl *on Amazon.com. Maher has a substantial career as a stand-up comedian, including eight HBO specials.*

Maher has consistently been listed in the Catholic League's Annual Report on Anti-Catholicism. He is often critical of organized religion and has described it as a "neurological disorder."

. . . .

I was Catholic until about thirteen. I didn't go to Catholic school, but I went to catechism on Sunday. We'd be dropped off and then my father would join us for church. My mother was Jewish and my father worked nights, so we didn't generally eat meals together. I don't remember us saying grace at the table.

In 1951 my parents got married and that was considered not cool by both their families. I really didn't sense that as a kid. When you're a kid, whatever is the routine you think is normal. That's how people get away with abusing children. Kids just think, "Ooh, that's what uncles and priests do. They touch me like that. I don't like it but . . ." I never really questioned why my mother didn't participate or go to church.

My father was a newsman. He was the real poster boy for the Irish Catholic, liberal American. His father was a union captain. They hated the Republicans. It was that very clanlike Irish thing.

My grandfather's sister voted Republican and it used to drive my father crazy. He would say, "Grace, you're living on Democratic coffers. You're living on the union pension of Uncle Lou." And she would say, "I don't care. I like Mr. Nixon."

When I was seven, a nun told me I was going to go to hell, because I was leaning on the pew in front of me. That was traumatic. I'll never forget those words, because it seemed so unreasonable. How could I reject them? That's another thing I hate about religion—that the proponents get to you when you're a defenseless child.

I didn't have much contact with priests personally, because the nuns were the ones who taught the catechism class. The nuns seemed mean. My father would always complain a lot about the priests— that their sermons weren't meaningful or that they spent too much time talking about how we had to fix the roof. He stopped going to church because he didn't agree at some point. He had a lot of guilt about it, so it wasn't the kind of thing he would've just announced. It was probably like, "Oh, we're not going this week. Dad doesn't feel well." Great! And next week, we weren't going again. I certainly wasn't going to object. It was like, if we weren't going, just shut up about it.

I don't have any Catholic guilt. I feel bad that my father had it. For him, it meant feeling guilty that he wasn't living up to the standards of what he had been taught was a good Catholic, which is ironic because it's a religion that is largely founded on making people feel guilt. That has a lot in common with the Jews.

I'm not one of those people who ever say, "I have no regrets." I don't know who those people are. I don't know what planet they're living on. But they need a slap upside the head, because you have regrets every day. It reminds me of that great John Lennon quote, when *Love Story* was out and the catch phrase was "Love means never having to say you're sorry." And he said, "Are you kidding? Love means having to say you're sorry every five minutes."

There's something every day I regret, even if it's small, but I handle that the way a modern person should—ethically. Ethicists are, to me, much more moral than religious people generally. Religious people can be moral, but morality is something that religion only occasionally stumbles upon.

I hate religion. It's the worst thing in the world. There's a giant groundswell for this opinion, but no one's said it in public. Maybe that's my destiny.

The more fundamentalist it is, the worse it is. Those people who fly planes into buildings because they think they're getting virgins in heaven are worse than Methodists who just go to church on Sunday. Religious moderates are enablers of religious fanatics. As long as it's legitimized to believe in nonsense, nonsense will have sway over people and look at the mess we're in.

I don't not believe in something, but I wouldn't say I believe in God. I learned the word "apatheist" from an ex-Mormon woman in Utah. She's a combination of apathy and atheist—apatheist, as in she doesn't care if there's a God and it shouldn't affect how you lead your life. I would agree with that, so it's sort of a moot question. One will never have the answers.

I've heard the Catholic League's not a big fan of mine. I won their award for being most critical of Catholics? No one insulted Catholics more than me and no one fucked kids more than the Catholic priests. I'll take insulting Catholics and they can have fucking kids. How about that?

Religion hurts people because it's so much death and destruction. It also diverts us. I think about what could be accomplished in this world if people wouldn't take the time and effort they've put into doing something that leads to absolutely nothing, like praying, and do something positive and tangibly good with it. It warps people's thinking.

There's no reason why you have to believe in God to do social justice work. Angelina Jolie does a lot of good work too, and we don't have to hear about Jesus. I have my own problems with missionaries, because I think there's something very evil about "Well, you want this sandwich, kid. Well, switch Gods first then we'll talk food." I'm breaking it down but basically, of course, it happens. It's a quid pro quo. I don't think necessarily they would hold back the sandwich before the kid agreed to believe in Jesus. I'm being comedic about it, but there is no doubt that the giving of aid and the inculcation of the new religion are put forth together.

Take a look at the Bible. Don't kill. I'm a big fan of that. The more I got into the Bible, the less I found even that to be true. You'd be hard pressed to find anything moral in a lot of the stories. Like Sodom and Gomorrah. The Old Testament is nothing but God as a total psychopath. He's constantly killing and wiping out everybody mostly for no damn good reason. That God is really awful.

Somebody did a calculation and added up all the people he killed. It's in the millions, whole towns, just genocide. Depending on whether he was feeling good about what the Jews were doing, he would wipe out their enemies or them.

Religion is basically selfish. It's not mostly about helping people. Its primary focus is your own salvation through Jesus Christ. For you to save your own ass after you die, you have to believe that this person was the son of God, came down here on a suicide mission, and then flew bodily back up to heaven where he rejoined his father who's also him. OK. I respect people as human beings. I don't wish them harm, but people who believe that can't have my intellectual respect.

I'm somewhat of a messenger. I do feel I have some destiny. Let's not get too religious with that. But maybe God is saying, "Bill, please, somebody tell them that I'm not what I'm cracked up to be. I can't take the pressure anymore. Please debunk me."

The last great intellectual frontier is to debunk religion.

If you go back through history, you'll be amazed at how many of the thinkers we all admire have quotes about religion that are more scathing than anything I could come up with—like Napoleon, Thomas Jefferson, and John Adams, just on and on. A hundred and fifty years ago, they thought Christianity was ending because science was becoming preeminent and answering the questions that religion had always answered.

I'd end the Church if I were pope.

Why can't we solve Iraq? It's because there's two tribes there who have a dispute about who succeeded the prophet Mohammed in the seventh century. That's why they're openly pulling each other out of each other's homes and slashing each other's throats. That's just powerful stupid. Until the world gets over shit like that, we're never going to solve global warming, terrorism, or anything.

Not in my lifetime do I see that going away, but I think we could make progress. I've been saying on television for fifteen years, get people to stop treating religion as a subject that is out of bounds. It deserves derision. It keeps people from mocking it by making them feel like it's the one thing that can't be mocked when it's the one thing that should most be mocked. We have to tear that barrier down.

I'm a crusader. I certainly have created enemies for a lot of reasons with lots of the things that I've said. But this is one of the touchiest issues there is. This is the last frontier. It's the last taboo.

E. J. DIONNE JR.

E. J. Dionne (b. April 23, 1952) is a senior fellow at the Brookings Institution and university professor in the Foundations of Democracy and Culture at Georgetown University. He defines for readers the strengths and weaknesses of competing political philosophies, and his analysis of American politics and trends of public sentiment is recognized as among the best in the business. He believes America is about to enter a new progressive era, a period of reform in government and renewed civic activism in our communities.

. . . .

I'm sure it's thanks to my parents that I've always seen faith as enriching and challenging, not oppressive. My mother and father acted in a way that showed their faith was important to them and that it demanded that we all behave with generosity and decency. So, despite all the problems in the Church, despite my own doubts, I stayed and experienced the Church as both nurturing and challenging.

I was raised in Fall River, Massachusetts, a factory town of about a hundred thousand people—85 percent Catholic, though we lived in the only Jewish neighborhood in town. It's a blessing that my parents made that choice. They were strong believers but also very open-minded about faith. My dad was a dentist in a working-class town. His dad was a housepainter whose business went under in the Depression. It was clear that many things in his life grew out of his faith. He organized all his fellow dentists to provide free care for poor kids. There were lots of kids in the town who wouldn't have seen a dentist otherwise.

He was active in St. Vincent De Paul and he was one of the two laypeople who assisted the pastor in running our church. So it was all very much a part of our lives. When my mother wasn't taking care of us, she was a teacher and a librarian. She was a very serious Catholic, read Merton, thought a lot about religious questions. She and our next-door neighbor, who was an Orthodox Jew, would often compare notes over the meaning of God and faith. When my dad died in 1968, my mom went back and taught at our parish school. So instead of having that sense that some people have that religion is hypocritical and narrow, I looked at how it affected the way they lived their lives and that was the attitude toward the faith that they passed on to me.

I was taught by nuns in grade school. My first lesson in civil rights came from Sister Genevieve, who was kicked out of Louisiana because she organized a biracial First Holy Communion service in the 1950s. She wasn't that stereotype that developed of "the radical nun." She simply thought: This is a Christian church and you don't segregate at First Communion.

Then I went to Portsmouth Priory. Most of the monks had pursued other work before they became monks. The headmaster was a physicist who worked on the A-bomb, another teacher was an actor in New York, then had been an Episcopal priest, and then became a Catholic and taught us the Bible. These were really smart people who made it impossible for me to accept the flawed but popular notion that if you're a person of faith, there must be limits on your intellectual capacity or imagination. I was immunized against many of the typical causes for rebellion against faith, both by my parents and by these extraordinary nuns and monks.

I always joke that I also probably stayed a Catholic because I went to Harvard from 1969 to 1973 and it was more rebellious to stay in the Church than to leave it. I thought leaving the Church meant being a class traitor, given the working-class roots of so many American Catholics. It was a time of real ferment. Students could pick from a number of masses. There was a High Mass for traditionalists; I liked the chaplain who ran what you might call the left-wing Mass. But I felt that it was a little separationist from the rest of the Church. I didn't like the idea that we'd cast ourselves as enlightened left-wingers who felt that the folks back at the regular parish didn't see the world as clearly as we did. So I found the perfect Mass for me, which was five o'clock Low Mass at the regular church. I found my way, between the radical church and the conservative church.

One should not overly psychoanalyze faith, but neither should one ignore personal influences. Clearly, where I grew up, politics, faith, and loving the Red Sox were all taken for granted. They were part of your life, and they were, on the whole, a good part of your life, even if the Red Sox could disappoint you, especially back then.

My parents were close to a lot of priests; they had very good friends in church so it wasn't an alien culture. I'd always say my late mom was very pro-priest and anticlerical at the same time. President Kennedy said that the bishops are Republicans and the nuns are Democrats. During the Kerry campaign, this group of nuns sent me a few buttons that portrayed the fires of hell in the middle, surrounded by the words "Catholic Democrat: Damned if you do, damned if you don't." The nuns are great.

The nuns, in many ways, were protofeminist. They built their own community and their own sense of power. In principle, their position was subordinate; in practice, they were essential to the functioning of the Church. The Church hasn't been the same since the decline in the number of nuns. They were the underpaid labor that undertook important work.

I became a liberal because I'm a Christian and a Catholic, but I grew up in a conservative family. From the time I was twelve or thirteen, I started rethinking things. My dad was very conservative but also very open-minded. He was against the Vietnam War before I was; we inverted the usual family pattern. My dad trained me for the life I pursued, because he encouraged argument. He gave me a subscription to the *New Republic* when I was thirteen. My mom was very interested and smart about politics too.

The Christian message about poverty, social justice, war, and violence had the effect of making me rethink a lot of things. Whenever people say Christians are naturally conservative, there are some circumstances where that is true, but for me it was quite the opposite. It struck me that to be a Christian had to involve thinking a lot about the poor or, as the Church has put it, about the "preferential option for the poor."

When I was fifteen or sixteen, Eugene McCarthy and Robert Kennedy had an enormous influence on the way I looked at the world. Kennedy's concerns about poverty, especially in the 1968 campaign, and the links he had with people like Cesar Chavez, were elemental, almost preintellectual, gut reactions to poor people and injustice.

Reflecting on the violence in Vietnam, I flirted with Catholic pacifism. When I registered for the draft in 1970, I checked a little box saying I was a pacifist and actually wrote a long Catholic pacifist statement to send to my draft board. I'll never forget sitting in my uncle's basement, after my dad had died, and reading and rereading it. I thought to myself, "I really like this, but I don't believe it." I wasn't a pacifist after all, so I withdrew my application for conscientious objection.

Again, the moral and intellectual resources of the Church—in this case, its teachings on just war—were invaluable in trying to sort through such questions. The people in the antiwar movement I most admired were the pacifists, including religious pacifists, because they had fewer illusions. They didn't pretend that what was then the North Vietnamese government was a great government. They opposed communist political repression but also worried that the American role in Vietnam was increasing the level of violence. There was an intellectual honesty to their witness. One of the reasons I could not bring myself to separate from the Church and faith, despite doubts and difficulties, is because so much of what the Church taught informed the conclusions I had reached.

When Abe Rosenthal came to Rome, I was covering the Vatican for the *New York Times*, and I helped him get a private audience with Pope John Paul II. Now, the truth is that Abe could have gotten that anyway, because he had been kicked out of Poland and won the Pulitzer Prize. I think the pope was aware that Abe had been a gutsy critic of the Polish Communist government. But Abe was happy that it all worked out. When we were walking across St. Peter's Square, I turned to Abe and said that I often told my friends in the Vatican that we have a lot in common because we worked for the only two institutions left in the world that claimed infallibility. Abe, bless him, didn't laugh.

If I were pope, I'd begin by convening people from the rich and poor countries—not just Catholics and not just religious people—to try to talk about what morally committed people can do in a sinful world full of injustice. The idea would be to put the Church in the center of an international conversation about what we can do about injustice and what role the Church could play. What does Catholic social justice teaching look like in a world that is globalized, where Marxism is largely dead? What is the peculiar role of Christianity and Catholicism in promoting justice and what does that mean? That might be the first thing I would do.

I wrote a column during the pedophile crisis that began, "Some of my best friends are priests . . ." I wanted to talk about them and talk about their anger. I argued that the paradox was that the Church's self-protective instinct hurt a lot of good priests by delaying necessary action. It was very upsetting to watch; there were really good bishops in that period who understood the moral and personal stakes and there were others who didn't.

Cardinal McCarrick was on to this much earlier than most. If you look at the record, he caught up with this issue before most people did. I heard an interesting story about McCarrick. There was a committee looking into a particular priest. The committee consisted of all priests except for one layperson who was a parent. Everybody on the committee said, "This is a great guy; it can't be true." And the parent said, "Look, maybe it is not true, but I am a parent, and I say, you've got to pull the guy." So the story, as I was told, is that McCarrick looked at the group and said, "Once in a while it's good we are not a democracy in the Church. He is right. I am going to pull the priest." It was a good example of a leader in the Church fighting the instinct of self-protection and facing up to what the scandal meant.

I have a theory that the Catholic Church's job is to make all of us feel guilty about something. Liberal Catholics should feel guilty and think hard about where they stand on abortion, family issues, and even stem cell research, which is a particularly hard one, for me at least. Conservative Catholics should worry about whether the policies they support are actually consistent with the well-being of the poor. If the Church makes us all think twice and three times about lots of issues, I think it is doing its job. When it appears to become an agent of one party in the political debate, it is very troubling.

SISTER JOAN CHITTISTER, O.S.B.

Joan Chittister (b. April 26, 1936) has been one of the Church's key visionary voices and spiritual leaders for more than thirty years. A Benedictine sister, she's an award-winning author and international lecturer on behalf of peace, human rights, women's issues, justice, and Church renewal.

. . . .

One day, in second grade, I'm told that Protestants don't go to heaven. I adored the second-grade teacher. Here was the rule. I was stunned. I was the only child in that class who didn't have a Catholic mother and Catholic father. My dad had died when I was three, and my mom married my stepfather, a Protestant. Every single year I was embarrassed on the first day of school when you signed the registration form, because every sister who ever taught me thought I'd made a mistake. Mixed marriages, that euphemism for crossing boundaries, just didn't exist and the local parish priest railed against them. He talked about parents whose children married non-Catholics and that they would be committing a sin if they went to the marriage of their own children. Dear God, help us. So I was living and being *dimmed* by all that.

I'm in religion class in the second grade and out it comes again in no uncertain terms. All the feelings I had felt, I now see are the rule. They are the law. Well, I raced out of school that night. I did not stay to clean the board. I didn't carry out the wastepaper basket. I didn't do papers for Sister. I just shot out of there. Why? Because in my family my stepfather and I got home at almost the same time every day; I came down the opposite side of the street from school; we walked in; everybody said hello, and the first question was always to me. What did you learn in school today, Joan? Well, this was the last thing I wanted to say in front of my father. This was big news. This was the biggest thing in school that day, as far as I was concerned.

I raced home, through the alley, over the fence, up to the house; my mother was in the kitchen doing dishes. I had to talk to her alone. She looked at me and said, "What happened to you? What'd you learn in school today that's got you so excited?" I looked at her, and I said right up, "Today I learned that Protestants don't go to heaven." And my mother didn't move. And then she said very quietly, "And what do you think about that, Joan?" And I said, "I think Sister is wrong." My mother said, "Why do you think Sister is wrong?" I thought for a minute and I said, "Sister doesn't know Daddy." She didn't have all the information, you see. Sister would never be wrong if somebody had told her all the information. So it was clear that she'd never seen anything like this. So my mother pulls me over and says, "What'd you say to Sister, Joan?" And I remember the shame, even telling this story now. I said, "I didn't say anything." My mother hugged me against her and said, "You're a very bright little girl, and I'm proud of you, Joan. You don't have to say anything now. You can tell Sister later." Honest to God, I think I've spent my whole life waiting to tell people how wrong this was.

I was affected by it negatively as a child and yet out of that negative experience and pressure came a positive drive to eliminate it from my own life—not to be part of any religion that somehow was the oppressor of others, of another religion. I had no power in the system, I had no voice in the system, but down deep in me, I knew.

And it's shaped my life. I spent my whole life with a foot on each side of the fence, and I absolutely refused to move either foot.

I was an only child when my mother became a widow at age twenty-one. She was getting ready to take me to the funeral home, and her brothers and sisters were having a fit. They kept saying, "You can't take that baby to a funeral home." And my mother, who was terribly undereducated but extremely bright, was furious, and she said to them, "You're out of your minds. What is she supposed to think? That her father just disappeared? That he left? That he's never coming back? She has to know he's dead. She has to be allowed to grieve him just the way the rest of us will." She took me. And she carried me up to the casket. She was holding me; I remember it. I had my little hands around her face; I could feel the wetness, and I knew. I looked down at the end of the casket and there sat the strangest-looking people I'd ever seen in my life all wrapped up in black. They had on these white-face kinds of things, and big sleeves, you couldn't see anything. Whatever these were, they were just sitting there like little round Russian nested dolls. And I said to my mother, "What are those?" And my mother said, "Joan, those are very special friends of God's, very special friends of your daddy's, and they give little girls' daddies to God. So they'll stay here. When angels come tonight, they'll say, 'This is Joan's daddy. He was a very good man. You take him straight to God so that he doesn't have to wait anyplace else.'"

Wow, I thought to myself, how could you do better than that? I made up my mind on the spot, and I spent the rest of my young life waiting to go to the monastery. When I got to the Catholic schools, I didn't experience any of the horror stories that people tell. I had wonderful sisters. They were funny, smart, kind. Most of the time, they were very just. I couldn't think of anything better to do with life.

If you equate holiness and spirituality with unspeaking deference; if you assume the role of the spiritual woman is some kind of support system rather than resource, then you diminish the whole tradition of religious life for women. I'm a Benedictine. This order is over fifteen hundred years old. There is no institution in the Church that's older except the Church itself. And these early monasteries of women had fine schools. The ones whose archives they even bothered to keep list the number of bishops who were taught in these schools. They were royal abbeys, meaning they had been founded by queens and princesses. They had fine lineage, good education, and a place of esteem in the society and in themselves when they entered; they were seeing something beyond the material.

Women got caught in the theology of sexuality rather than the theology of humanity. When celibacy was imposed on men in the thirteenth century, that's when the cloister was imposed on women. As the Church became more institutionalized, women had more cloister imposed on them, both within the Church and in society in general. No good woman went out alone. No good woman went out at night. No good woman functioned on her own in society.

So, today, you say to women, yes, you're right about all that his-

tory; yes, you're right about all that theology; and yes, it's wrong.
Now, what it takes are strong women whose relationship with God is
so profound, so stable, and so clear in terms of their own call to make
this world a better place. It's a call to us now to reverse this kind of
subservience as a substitution for sanctity and to help women regain
and develop their rightful place in the mind of God for the sake of
the people of God. We can't just take it and we can't just abandon it.
It's too valuable, too valued, too beautiful a life in the tradition to
simply destroy it.

I grew up at the tail end of the Catholic Youth Organization
movement. It may have been a kind of a carryover from the Church's
participation in the labor movement and the whole question of just
wages and unions after the war. I went to the Benedictines and in our
academy the whole notion of "I'm a citizen of two worlds" was just
part of the air you breathed. It was the ethos of the place. The as-
sumption was that if you were a young Catholic woman you were
dedicated to the development of the poor. Quite frankly, at that period, the poor to whom you were devoted would've been largely
Catholic. We were still coming out of that "Irish need not apply" period, and Catholics definitely needn't apply. It was a response to the
anti-Catholicism of the time, but most of all to the awareness after
the war that there was a poverty problem in the United States.

We're Benedictines so we pray together three times a day to
psalms and scripture. The interesting thing is that the rule of Benedict says that prayers should be brief, so that those words can wash
through you all day long, so that your mind is somehow attuned to
these messages and their effect on your own life. The Benedictine
lives a life of contemplation and meditation at all times. We'll read
the Bible through and then we start over again. The scriptures become then the heartbeat of your life. They're the pulse that goes
through the spiritual body of a Benedictine community, and it becomes the very breath you breathe.

After Vatican II, religious orders were going through all of this
change and there was a great deal of confusion. There was a lot of

polarization, uncertainty, anger, and concerns about what sisters were going through in this period while they were trying to adapt life to a new society, and a lot was swirling around the whole issue of the habit. Should you wear the habit? What's the habit about? And it was a big thing for me, because I loved the tradition and I loved the order and certainly didn't want to lose it. I can honestly remember the day I said to myself, "Joan, it comes down to this. Are you or are you not a Benedictine in the bathtub?"

The community always says that the only thing that's gotten me through is my own sense of humor, however bad it may be. It may be outrageous but it's clear. What might have been my greatest human achievement has been the ability to make the transition from the trappings of a thing to the essence. Of really discovering that if you want the religious life, you don't lose it by living life as a normal and full human being. There's an old monastic story that says something like this: When a drunk goes into a cell, the cell becomes a tavern, and when the monk goes into a tavern, the tavern becomes a cell. We create the environment that we're in.

Change really doesn't happen from the top. Not in the Catholic Church. It happens from the bottom and it happens over long periods of time. The whole notion that the Catholic Church doesn't change is only said by people who don't know history. It's a changing body, but the problem is that some people get chewed up in that long, slow process. That is the sin of the Church. But that is what happens when you're the vanguard or articulator of any idea in a developmental process.

The first thing I'd do is to bring women into all arenas of the Church, all areas of authority and idea development. I'd make the Church a universal church instead of a male church, and I'd do it overnight. Why? That's the only way that you're going to hear and develop the full theology of the Church. Don't talk to me about social justice and do nothing about the case of women. Don't talk to me about the sanctity of marriage and do nothing about the training of men and male attitudes toward the way the family goes together.

Don't talk to me about justice and assume that half of the human race can simply carry the injustice of the other half and "offer it up." I won't go there.

I'm far closer to the ideas of Teilhard de Chardin. Chardin says that when we die we enter into the stream of life. I don't know what that is. I presume that there may well be a consciousness that goes with it, but I don't find that necessary. Let me put it this way: Life has been good. Life is a great gift, and I don't believe that something this great was meant to go to nothing. I also believe that we spend too much time in our puny little minds. The first thing we say is God is all mystery. No one can know God. Then we explain to you quite precisely what God is about and everything God thinks and all the rules that God wants kept. There's not a single message about narcotics in the Bible. Now you think God would have been concerned about that. I have a funny feeling that we do God as much disservice as we do service.

DORIS KEARNS GOODWIN

Doris Kearns Goodwin (b. January 4, 1943) is a presidential historian who has written award-winning books on Johnson, Kennedy, Lincoln, and Franklin Delano Roosevelt and is currently an analyst for NBC News. A lifelong baseball fan, she grew up in Rockville Centre, a religiously diverse New York suburb.

. . . .

The reason why Catholicism remains such an emotional force in all of us is that the memories are so intense. They all tend to be stories, in a certain sense, about what happened when you were a young Catholic child and had all of those notions filling your head about heaven and hell, purgatory and limbo. Growing up in Rockville Centre, we had this beautiful cathedral for a church, which was part of the magic of it.

Preparing for my first confession, I was terrified that I'd committed two sins that related to baseball, which was my other passion beyond the Church when I was growing up. The first sin had to do with the fact that the Dodgers' catcher, Roy Campanella, was coming to speak in our hometown on Long Island. It was announced that he was speaking in a Protestant church, which sent shivers down my spine. I believed that stepping foot in a Protestant church was committing a mortal sin. When I walked over the threshold of the church that night, my legs trembled beneath me. I was worried that I'd traded the life of my everlasting soul—at seven years old—for that one night with Roy Campanella.

That sin still rested on me when a couple of days later two trains collided at the station in my town. I began to discern from this horrible calamity the opportunity for my redemption. We learned in catechism that if you were present when somebody was dying, and if no priest was at hand, you could, as a layperson, baptize the wounded. They could go to heaven and your sins would be wiped out. Never had I needed to have my sins wiped out more than with Roy Campanella on my soul. I had been practicing baptisms on my doll for months in hopes that I might be needed. The only thing that prevented me from the humiliation of lifting the blankets at the train station and asking seriously injured people if they wanted me, a seven-year-old, to baptize them, was that the train station was right across from the church so there were plenty of priests on the scene.

I still had this sin to deal with when I went to my first confession. I made the decision to tell the priest about it right away, figuring that if I could get it over with, then maybe I'd be able to relax. He told me exactly what my father had said, that it wasn't a religious service so it wasn't a sin. But then he said, "And what else, my child?" I tried to hide the other sin relating to baseball in the mix of talking in church several times, disobeying my mother five times, wishing harm to others, and telling fibs. Unfortunately, he asked me, "On whom did you wish harm?" I had to admit that I wished that various players—all of our competitors—would break arms, legs, and ankles so that the Brooklyn Dodgers could win their first World Series. The priest said to me, "How often did you make these terrible wishes?" I had to admit, every night when I said my prayers. I explained that if God were powerful enough to spread these injuries around, he could cure everyone the moment that the Dodgers won the World Series. Fortunately, it turned out that the priest was a baseball fan. He said, "I promise you someday they will win fairly and squarely. You do not need to wish harm on others players." As I left the confessional, he said, "Say a special prayer for all Brooklyn Dodgers."

Another time, I was going to a game at Ebbets Field, and Gil Hodges, the Dodgers' first baseman, was in a terrible slump. People in parishes all over Brooklyn were praying for him. He was a beloved player, but he just couldn't hit day after day and week after week. I had won a St. Christopher's medal blessed by the pope for having known the seven deadly sins. I was down to the finals and was pitted against a parochial school student. I remember having the feeling that most of the audience and the sisters would pray for her to win instead of me. She got most of them, but she didn't remember gluttony. So I won this medal. It used to be believed that St. Christopher was the patron saint of travel and he would help you travel safely. I brought it to the park with me, and I thought that if I gave it to Gil Hodges then he would be able to travel safely around the bases and get out of his slump. He took it and said he was grateful—he was such a gracious man. I must have looked ridiculous with this medal. The next day he hit well, and I was certain I was responsible.

There's an epilogue. In 2001 I met Hodges's widow and she told me she still had the St. Christopher's medal. It was such a happy moment.

Because my mother had been so sick, suffering a series of little heart attacks before the one that killed her when I was fifteen, there was a sense of sadness as to why God had not allowed her to be healthy. I don't remember being angry at God, but just feeling sad about our whole family's situation. Before she died, my instinct was to pray that she would get better, so I definitely had a sense of trying to talk to God.

Her death didn't turn me against religion or God. When you're an adolescent, the primary reaction is feeling as if you're in a different place from other people. Fortunately, that didn't last too long because I really loved school and had a lot of friends.

I remember talking with Rose Kennedy about the early deaths of four of her nine children and what it'd be like if they could come back to life. She was convinced that they would still choose the lives they'd been given—even though they had been short—because of the productivity, fulfillment, and adventure of those lives. This was really quite emotional for me to hear; it struck me as such a wonderful way to think about it.

I suppose she found enormous solace in this idea. It makes complete sense to prefer a full life, even if it's a shorter number of years, since it's all preparation for the next world. I couldn't find that same sense of solace when I thought about my own kids.

My Catholic upbringing influenced my decision to stay home and care for my kids when they were young. There's one story from when the kids were little that I specifically recall. I was working endlessly on the Kennedy book, but it hadn't come out yet, and I wasn't teaching anymore. I was at a cocktail party and somebody said, "Whatever happened to Doris Kearns anyway?" They didn't realize that I could hear. I wanted to hit them and say, "I have three boys; that's what has happened to me." Family was my priority.

Now my children are in their late twenties and thirties, leading lives of service to their communities.

I'd like to believe that the combination of some Jewish traditions and rituals and some Catholic ones has allowed them to become the kinds of human beings they are.

There's something about the rituals of the Church that are so beautiful. The act of shared celebrations, shared moments of sadness, and then coming away from that to happy celebrations that make you feel connected to something larger than a family or a neighborhood. You're connected to a community, a church, and therefore a country.

Part of the passion for history is the great pleasure of catapulting yourself back to another era and imagining what it was like to walk around during the Civil War, World War II, or the 1960s. In the Catholic Church there are different levels that you're living on—personal life, religious life, life on this earth, and a life later on. It gives you a sense of dimension, and that's what history does as well.

Abraham Lincoln had a real obsession with being remembered after he died. The interesting question is, does the deep Catholic faith or a belief in afterlife soften that need? It seems in Lincoln's case not believing or not being sure that there was an afterlife made him even more passionate to do something. Otherwise you were just dead. That is why when his first love, Ann Rutledge, died at twenty-two, he couldn't bear it when the rain fell on her grave. I think that would make it even more compelling to accomplish something if you didn't believe that one's soul goes somewhere.

Some people were worried that Lincoln had never joined an organized church and that he didn't go to church regularly on Sundays. One of his friends said that if you judged Lincoln by organized religion and the rituals of the Church, he might not appear a religious man. But if you judged him by the ethical and moral values by which he led his life—compassion, kindness, sensitivity, and empathy—then he was as religious as anyone else could possibly be.

Religion helps people develop moral, ethical, and emotional values. That's what you're looking for when you look at public figures. Franklin Roosevelt chose brilliantly on the eve of D-day when he had to figure out what to tell the American people about the fact that our troops were beginning to finally invade northern France and that there might be many deaths. He chose the form of a prayer, and it was perfectly toned at that point in time to do so.

JAMES CARROLL

James Carroll (b. January 22, 1943) is a renowned author, novelist, and columnist. He served as Catholic chaplain at Boston University from 1969 to 1974 and then left the priesthood to become a writer. Carroll still worships in the Catholic tradition, while much of what he believes would mark him as a reform-minded Catholic in the spirit of John XXIII.

. . . .

I was brought up when Catholicism was very rigid, very defensive, and very clearly defined. The Counter-Reformation still held. We knew exactly what was expected of us. There was something deeply consoling about that world. I think it was especially consoling for an immigrant population in a culture that felt somewhat hostile. So we were Americans, but first we were Catholics. Add to that being Irish. Irish Catholicism gave us a strong sense of identity and of clarity about moral questions. We knew what was right; we knew what was wrong. We had a way to deal with the guilt we felt when we did something wrong—that constellation of sacraments, centered on confession. All of this was psychologically bracing, even though there was a kind of punishing theology behind it. Still there was nothing to compare with that crystal clear feeling attached to coming out of confession on a Saturday afternoon.

The trouble with that world of transgression, guilt, and even forgiveness, such as it was, is that it had very little to do with who Jesus Christ actually was. The threat of damnation overhanging Catholic life was dehumanizing, and even the relief from it—"absolution"—was dehumanizing in subtle ways that we were barely aware of. A system based on threatened doom made us frightened of our own freedom, and it made us infantile when it came to making choices. We yielded our adult responsibility to the "father." The hierarchical system was deadening to the conscience, to the spirit, and to the imagination. So with all of this as background, perhaps you can appreciate what a tremendous liberation it was—the defining Catholic event that took place when I was a young man.

That was the unexpected arrival of Pope John XXIII. It was the magnificent moment of my life and it changed everything for me. It enabled me to really embrace Catholicism in a much deeper way.

What made John's arrival doubly powerful for Americans, of course, was the synchrony of the arrival of the Kennedy family—a new way of being Catholic, a new way of being American. Pope John and President Kennedy were partners in an astounding, exhilarating, life-changing event. For Catholics, the renewal pointed in one direction, which was to the figure of Jesus, on whom this whole Christian experience is based. I had the privilege as a young man of actually discovering Jesus in a real way. I did that in a seminary, my first step toward becoming a priest. A step I took while Pope John and John Kennedy were in their prime.

We believe in the tradition that authority comes from God. Traditionally, for Catholics, that has meant that it comes through the bishops in the Church. The hierarchy of the Church mustn't be questioned. But at the same time, the Church has always affirmed that the authority of truth is essentially mysterious, and therefore must constantly be discovered. Perhaps traditional authority isn't what we first thought it was. We really never know, for sure, who God is, or what God means; we don't really know for sure who Jesus was, what Jesus meant. The proclamation of truth, whether about God or Jesus, is mysterious. Truth is elusive; therefore authority proclaiming the truth is ambiguous. Such mystery and ambiguity lead to inconsistencies in Church teaching and behavior. In Catholicism it is not only revolutionaries who question authority. Down through the centuries, because of inbuilt mystery and ambiguity, the Church questions its own authority. We've seen that, for example, in the tension between the popes exercising authority alone, and the bishops exercising authority in councils.

The irony of our lifetime is that while we still say that the pope is infallible and that he has supreme authority in the Church, what is our source for saying that? How do we know the pope is over the council? Because the council said so! The First Vatican Council promulgated the doctrine of infallibility and said the pope is supreme. There is a paradox there, and the Second Vatican Council began to grapple with it, an all but explicit challenge to the solitary supremacy of the pope. The Second Vatican Council affirmed the principle of collegiality, a mitigation of papal supremacy. That, more than anything, is why the reforms of the Second Vatican Council have been resisted in certain Catholic circles since the council's end. The Church's own structure of organization has a democratic and self-critical principle to it.

Anybody who says that Church belief is timeless and will never change doesn't know the history of the Church. The Church is constantly changing its beliefs by constantly understanding them in fresh ways, which is inevitable with human beings on the earth. The genius of the Catholic Church, and key to its survival as an institution, is the fact that its structure, even if implicitly, is built on self-criticism, which at any given point the Church itself might deny. That denial too is evidence of change, for at multiple times in the past, the principle of change has been affirmed. So living with these tensions and contradictions is key to being a Catholic.

That Catholic identity is centrally important to me, which is why I remain clearly and firmly a Catholic. I worship in the Catholic tradition and honor the Catholic institution, even while much of what I believe would disqualify me from a more rigid notion of what it is to be a Catholic. I don't believe in the infallibility of the pope, for example. So what is the Church to do with someone like me? Another ingenious aspect of the Catholic Church is that it's very slow to excommunicate. In our tradition, excommunication is very grave, and it shouldn't be undertaken lightly. That is why certain American bishops made such fools of themselves during the 2004 presidential campaign when they began talking about excommunicating politicians who didn't take a particular stand on certain questions. I think those bishops were being untrue to the Catholic tradition.

My beloved Roman Catholic tradition is full of things I reject. I am appalled by its contempt for women. The fact that Catholic bishops continue to play their games—male apostles, "fathers," God as "He"—all to avoid ordaining women as priests is unbelievable. I am amazed that the Catholic people aren't up in arms about it. Discrimination by gender equals discrimination by race. Would the Catholic people tolerate a prohibition of blacks from the priesthood? Of course not! Why do they tolerate the prohibition of women?

I study the Bible, taking it as the revelation that we creatures are beloved, that the One who loves us is our Creator—loves us into existence. God's covenant with Israel made this real, and Jesus makes it available to me. I have a strong connection to Jesus and to the community that remembers him.

I'm not what anyone would recognize as a pious person, but I do have an intense sense of connection to God. I don't worry about any particular notions of afterlife, but I believe that my connection to God is unbreakable, even by death. Who is God to me? God is beyond my capacity to express. God is unknown. God is beyond the horizon, but what I know about God I know from Jesus and from the community that remembers him.

When I go to Mass, it's for a very simple act of accepting bread and tasting wine in the company of other people who are very different from me. The story we tell is what makes us a community. I can go to any Catholic church and feel at home.

In the 1960s the Church's obligation to be a beacon of social justice became clear in a fresh way, mostly from the witness of people like Martin Luther King Jr. and other non-Catholic Christian ministers, who began to insist in powerful ways that you couldn't preach the Gospel without attention to the question of justice. The American Catholic Church's commitment to justice had been powerful, but it'd been narrowly centered on the Church's own people, immigrants, and workers. The Church long resisted religious discrimination, and it was a powerful advocate of the labor movement.

But it's one of the great shames of an otherwise powerful history to discover again and again that the Catholic Church in America was indifferent to the scandal of slavery, which in the nineteenth century was the great question of social justice. The Catholic Church wasn't there. In the aftermath of slavery, the Catholic Church was missing again.

Something in the Church's understanding of the call to justice changed in the 1960s, not just in this country but in the Vatican as well. Even before the civil rights movement, and then the peace movement, I think that the great change in Catholic moral awareness came about when Catholics confronted Church failures during World War II. Catholics recognized, with many other Christians, the grievous failure of the Church to seriously and effectively oppose Hitler. And Catholics confronted, equally, the harsh fact that Hitler couldn't have nearly succeeded in his genocidal campaign against the Jewish people if it hadn't been prepared for by centuries of Christian and Catholic anti-Judaism. This revolution in moral awareness prepared all Catholics, from the pope to the laity, to understand in a new way the Church's obligation to be firmly on the side of those who suffer from injustice, and firmly opposed to war.

The moment I was most proud to be a Catholic was when John Paul II at the millennium insisted that we couldn't cross the threshold into the new century without a serious act of repentance for the failures of the Church. And Pope John Paul did that against the advice of his conservative inner circle. This man acknowledged the gravest failures of the Church, an instance of moral reckoning that, to consider another example, the United States of America has never come close to accomplishing.

I think the catastrophe of the Holocaust broke one terrible tradition in the Church—its anti-Semitism. The Church is confronting this. It's not doing a perfect job, but it isn't doing a bad job either. The catastrophe of the priestly child abuse scandal is also forcing the Church to confront the corruption of the clerical culture. The abuse scandal shows that the clerical culture is in collapse. Laypeople are asserting themselves more and more. Conservative Catholics place their hopes in the apparent conservatism of Catholics in Latin America, Asia, and Africa, but it is condescending to assume that third-world Catholics are any more inclined to submit to autocratic and unaccountable authorities than Americans and Europeans are. After all, it is out of Latin America that liberation theology comes. And by "liberation" they mean liberation. I think the empowerment of laypeople in the Catholic Church is part of the worldwide movement of empowerment of people generally, what shaped the twentieth century and will continue in the twenty-first.

A Catholic layperson can claim such power simply by refusing to leave the Church just because those in charge define membership narrowly, in terms of subservience. A Catholic can continue to claim Catholic identity even while disagreeing powerfully with those who assert their exclusive right to define Catholic identity. There is no one meaning of Jesus, for example. There are many meanings of Jesus, which is why there are twenty-seven books about him in the New Testament, and not just one. The Church is the place where these various meanings get articulated. Down through the century those articulations have changed. They are changing today.

Ideally, those in authority serve as guides and resources for change. But when they tell us that the process of change is wrong, or when they tell us there is only one meaning to Catholic faith, we say politely, no.

The Church's position on condom use for protection against HIV and AIDS may be the single worst betrayal of which I'm aware in my recent lifetime as a Catholic. Think of those pleading Catholics in Africa—laypeople, priests, and bishops—asking the Vatican over the last ten or fifteen years to reconsider this. AIDS is decimating Africa, and what is the response of the Catholic Church? To let go of limbo so that all those dead children can get to heaven? The presumption of Pope John Paul II going to Africa and reasserting the Church's prohibition of condoms to a vast audience, many of whom were infected, was appalling.

There are many Catholics who, for good reasons of conscience, when they divorce, want to observe the Church's regulation on divorce and remarriage. The Church's rejection of divorce begins with Jesus' own sayings about the indissolubility of marriage, and its annulment system begins as an attempt to respond pastorally to those whose marriages have ended. But the system doesn't work. It often puts Catholics in the tragic position of denying who they are and what they've done. There are many Catholics who are simply not going to do that, and that refusal is a good thing. Such resistance puts pressure on the Church to reconsider the bizarre dead-end annulment system they've created.

To pretend, in seeking an annulment, that "there was no marriage" is dishonest, but it's also an insult to the good people who get caught in a marital bind—including children. That the Catholic people increasingly decline to participate in the annulment system is what'll make the system change. The Church should simply acknowledge that the context in which Jesus is remembered as forbidding divorce has changed. Divorce can be a necessary course of action, and the Church should accommodate that, as many Catholic laypeople already have.

I think, similarly, that people don't go to confession to confess the "sin" of contraception. Catholic people have made their choices about such things, and the hierarchy is being entirely left behind. The Catholic people, in other words, are really changing the Church quite powerfully, simply by continuing to affirm their identities as Catholics while also affirming their responsibilities for their own lives and choices.

The structure of the Church hasn't caught up with this new reality, but it will. I'm confident that it will.

DONNA BRAZILE

RON AIRA

Donna Brazile (b. December 15, 1959) is founder and managing director of Brazile and Associates, LLC. A chair of the Democratic National Committee's Voting Rights Institute and an adjunct professor at Georgetown University, she's a senior political strategist and former campaign manager for Gore–Lieberman 2000—the first African American to lead a major presidential campaign.

. . . .

Like many natives of the New Orleans area, I was raised in the Catholic Church and steeped in its culture and values. I really enjoyed my early experiences of going to church. Not only did I enjoy the masses in Latin—although I couldn't understand one word— I enjoyed the rituals and the feeling I had as a little girl of being in the Catholic Church. I started going to Mass at the age of three. Back then, we were told to sit in the back pews on the left-hand side. That was the little section designated for colored people. This was long after the signs had been removed. But it was custom, so no one violated the agreement. It was always just sit in the back, shut up, and be quiet. This was 1963.

Our Lady of Perpetual Health was located right next to the second set of train tracks running through town. The first set separated the blacks and whites, and the second set separated the working poor from the middle class. The church was on the line between both race and economics; there were poor whites in that church because they lived on the other side of the tracks, and of course poor blacks and working-class people. You got a chance to interact with people of other races and backgrounds. Nevertheless, I realized even as a little girl that my place in church was sitting in the back on the left-hand side.

By the time I turned six or seven, I had a pretty clear view of what I wanted to be. I wanted to be a priest. I loved going to church. I loved the fact that my mother would put fresh ribbons in our hair and my grandmother would always iron our dresses. We looked neat and wonderful, all nine of us walking down the train tracks to church every Sunday morning. Our mother would march us out after serving us the best breakfast of the week: grits, eggs, and either bacon or sausage. She'd give us a nickel to put in the collection box, and we'd stop at Burton's Pharmacy to break the nickel down to pennies, telling ourselves that God would forgive us for giving him just two cents because we wanted three cents to buy penny candy.

Around this time, things were improving a little bit on race relations. Or at least I figured they were because we started moving to the center pews. Still in the back, mind you, but before long we gradually moved closer and closer toward the middle of the church.

Then something happened. I don't know if it was Martin Luther King's assassination or what, but all of a sudden we were no longer expected to sit in the back. We could sit *anywhere* in the church. By the time I went through my First Holy Communion, I was right up front. That's where I always wanted to be anyway. I wanted to see everything the priest was doing. *I wanted to be a priest.* I knew God wanted it too. So I'd get to church very early to get that special seat. When I went home the day after finally reaching the very first pew, I announced to my mother, "I know what I want to be when I grow up. I want to be a priest!"

My mother said, "Little girls can't be priests."

No one had told me up until that moment, when I was able to finally sit up front, that little girls couldn't be priests.

Here I had been working my way up in the church—from sitting in the back on the left-hand side to getting in the middle to creeping forward to the front—to going to special First Holy Communion classes and answering the questions correctly, and learning just about everything I could about the Church. I could read scripture. I knew the Bible. I quizzed the nuns. I memorized all the moves the priest made throughout Mass.

For heaven's sake and mine, why couldn't I be a priest? I wanted to speak in Latin. I wanted to wear the robes. I wanted to earn the ultimate seat in the front of the church. *Why can't little girls be priests?*

My mother told me I could be a nun. A nun? I didn't see nuns as having that big of a role other than teaching classes on weekends about our faith. They didn't break bread. And they sure didn't bless the water (wine, but who knew since children were forbidden from tasting it). I didn't want to be a nun. I decided I'd just have to find another way to serve the Church.

I still go to church. I have an excellent relationship with my priest. We talk. A lot. He knows my personal differences with the Church. I won't exploit them, but I'm clear about my beliefs and my values. The values that I've obtained from the Church I carry in my everyday life: serving others, fighting for justice and equality, being there for those in need, and not turning my back on people who are suffering. Those are the Christian Catholic values that I'll always uphold and preserve. As it turns out, I learned that you don't have to be a priest to be a servant of God.

It was a dynamic time to be growing up in the Deep South. There was something happening all the time, and my family was engaged. The values of social justice and fairness were drilled into us. Every day we heard the same stories, primarily the Sermon on the Mount. Every day we had the same doctrine preached over and over: to serve, to serve, to serve. And, of course, there was the endless message of giving back to one's community and to love coupled with the eternal admonition to love thy enemies. I used to think, "Can we skip over that because we have too many enemies?"

The virtues were drilled into us in church, CCD classes, after-school classes, and by our parents and grandparents. Anytime they thought we were being selfish or self-centered, they reminded us of Jesus' sacrifice and love for everyone—poor and rich alike. My mother made a practice of not throwing anything away. And she didn't allow us to either. We'd ask, "Why shouldn't we throw it away?" And she'd always reply, "Because there are people starving around us. They need things. There are people without clothes. They need those clothes you want to throw away. I could make bread pudding if you don't want that bread. I could make jambalaya if you don't eat that rice." I used to sit there and think, "Wow! There are people less fortunate than us? How could that be? They must be in Africa!" She was right. They were often living right behind us or next door.

My mother always kept an open door to those less fortunate than us. They could always come in and get a bite to eat or a few hand-me-down clothes. Everything I owned was hand-me-down. I had hand-me-down dresses, shoes, T-shirts, and play clothes, but I also had to hand things down as well. After we handed them down to each other, we handed them around to others because that was part of the Church teachings.

If you were Catholic, the nuns would come to school after classes ended and they'd conduct special classes to prepare us for our First Holy Communion. I didn't think twice about this until I was a senior in high school. I finally wondered, how did that happen? Growing up, the connection seemed natural: public school, church, and the community center. There was no separation.

If you drink from the fountain of Catholic faith, it becomes a large part of who you are—the spirit of being present in everyday life and the knowledge of having the saints on your side to comfort and guide you.

I'll never forget when I was coming out of college and had a job all set at Procter & Gamble. I told my mom that I had to put it off for a year. I said, "I'm gonna take this job, Mom. God knows I can't wait to move to Cincinnati and feel all that cold, blowing snow. But I have an opportunity to go to Washington, D.C., to help make Martin Luther King's birthday a national holiday." My mother said, "Don't you think you need the money and don't you think you need to get that job?" I told her, "I will, but first I gotta do this."

It was a calling. I was torn between making money and doing what I believed was the right thing to do. It's still with me. Recently, I was offered a huge contract—forty-five thousand dollars a month—to consult and lobby for a major company. I wanted that contract, but I had to pass. I'd be selling out the very people I'd want to help represent—the workers. I couldn't be on the side of a corporation that cheated its workers by not providing health benefits. That's the Catholic Church. It's part of who you are.

I believe that the calling we receive when we're young is to *serve*. If God puts you in a position to, say, be on TV or radio or to help work on a political campaign, it's to champion those issues that are near and dear to you and God. For me, they're equality and justice.

I've always been able to square the Church's opposition to a candidate's stance on certain issues with where the candidate stands on the broad range of issues concerning the Catholic Church. I didn't agree with Al Gore on the death penalty. I'm opposed to the death penalty. Yet I was able to work on his presidential campaign and the two campaigns of Bill Clinton.

As far as the pro-life/pro-choice issue, as a woman I feel as strongly about my body as I do about an unborn child in someone else's body. I believe in the sanctity of life, but I also believe that I must preserve the choice. As the result of being a descendant of slaves, where my ancestors had no control over their reproductive health or even access to age-appropriate reproductive health information, I believe it's essential for women to have a choice.

The Church taught me about free will and free choice, so as a Catholic I figure I can make this decision. I'm a fierce advocate for my own values. I know that Jesus loves sinners and that he said, "Come to me and I shall set you free." I also have the ability to repent and ask for forgiveness.

Read Matthew 14, when Jesus said, "Be not afraid." I'm always delighted when I hear the priest read a scripture and then give a lecture that goes back to the original teachings of Christ and not this form of Christianity that people exploit. "Be not afraid" was part of the theme of the civil rights movement.

When I used to listen to the priest give the scripture in church, I'd later ask for him to write it down. Then I'd go back to do my own research and I'd have all sorts of questions as to whether or not he got it right.

I loved the Bible because it was something I could champion and use to help build a case for the causes I worked on. It was a book for warriors. I spent almost two years going to church every day with Reverend Jesse Jackson during his historic bid for the presidency in 1984. At first I thought, "This man is going to transform me into a Baptist." But I ended up turning out more Catholic, because I wanted to go back to the regular routine of the Church.

My favorite Bible passages depend on what I'm going through. Right now I'm studying this whole period of time when Jesus lowered his disciples into rough water knowing that it was a test of their faith. Being premenopausal, I'm trying to understand a little bit more about that period. What is the lesson that I need to learn as I try to get through this next passage in life?

There are other portions of the Bible that I go to depending on my mood, my spirit, and what I'm experiencing. The Bible always guides me. I own about five different copies.

I think that as a child you're more formal in your prayers. You get all these different prayer books that give you instructions. As an adult, I have two ways of praying. First, I go to St. Mattress. This is when I'm lying on the bed and I feel a need to have a conversation with God. He is never busy. There are other times when I get on two knees. I call that Bedside Baptist, because I'll actually pray aloud in my house. If anybody hears me, so be it. I have to have this cry because I need it. It's why Psalm 28 is so powerful: "When I called on you, you answered me." It's true that God answers prayers.

I think we're all recycled spirits in human bodies and part of our duty and our journey in this physical phase of our life is to complete God's will here on earth. Our good works, our deeds, and our service are put into action not here but in the beyond.

I fear the experience of dying. But, as I grow older, I see it differently. You're not just here in the physical, you're here spiritually— and the dead never leave you. They visit you *often.* I come home some days and it feels like my house is more like a bar. Then I know that they were there all day, partying, talking to one another, and carrying on. I finally decided that it's better to join them than fight them, so when I wrote my will a couple of years ago, I put my money where my beliefs are: Here is ten thousand dollars. Spend it joyfully and celebrate my life. I want my family and friends to party after my burial. I want them to tell some Donna stories—the good ones that have you on the floor laughing. I want them to tell the truth and enjoy being in my company—even if they cannot see me with their physical eyes. I'll be there in spirit, partying along with them and dancing to the music.

I haven't connected spiritually with Pope Benedict XVI. Nevertheless, if you walk into my office, you'll find him on my wall. And, of course, I've got a crucifix over my front door and over my bedroom door. I'm a traditional Catholic. I make no excuses. Yes, I still curse and drink wine, but I do have my crucifixes up. I go to confession and ask for forgiveness.

I've tried to reconcile Hurricane Katrina as God's trying to tell the world something—not just New Orleanians, but the world.

The Bible says that you've got to find the blessings in the storms of life. I still haven't figured out the blessings of hurricanes. It's so personal for me and for so many others to see your entire family lose everything and be dislocated.

Throughout the first two weeks of that ordeal, there were people who didn't have anything but the clothes on their backs. The most important thing lots of people wanted was their family Bible. They wanted to rebuild their lives first on their faith. They were all glad to have made it through the storm, grateful to survive. The bitterness didn't come until months later. The anger didn't appear until almost a year later when they realized that not only were they left to die by their government but that their government wasn't keeping its promise to help them get their lives back in order.

While my family was lost (temporarily, thank God) in the midst of that storm, I relied on St. Anthony, the most powerful saint I could think of, the patron saint of finding what is lost. St. Anthony, I hoped and prayed, could find my father and my sisters and my brothers. Day after day of not knowing if anyone in my family was dead or alive, I relied on him to give me strength. That period and the painful months that followed it was one of the greatest tests of faith my family has ever faced. It was also a test of faith for our city, which was built on a foundation of faith. Now, as always, the people of New Orleans, no matter where they now live, get up on Sunday morning and go to church. Their faith, now as always, is rock solid.

NANCY PELOSI

*As the highest-ranking elected woman in American history,
Nancy Pelosi (b. March 26, 1940) broke the marble
ceiling to become the first woman to serve as Speaker of
the House of Representatives in 2007. She is second in
the line of presidential succession.*

. . . .

When my mom asked if I wanted to be a nun, I said I'd rather be a priest.

We grew up in a devoutly Catholic, deeply patriotic home, where we were proud of our Italian American heritage and very committed to the Democratic Party. I was the youngest of six and the only girl. My mother thought the most wonderful way to profess your faith if you were a girl was to become a nun. The nuns were always wonderful, but the power was with the priest. I always thought that nuns should be able to be priests. That's one of the things the Catholic Church is going to have to face.

We profess our faith and then we act upon it. One way to do this is through public service. In our case, the manifestation was the Democratic Party. The Gospel of Matthew really sounded like a platform for the Democrats. So it was a logical extension of faith and politics and also of a family in politics. When I became a mother I could see that if I wanted the best possible future for my children, other children would have to have greater opportunities. I saw that as an extension of faith and family, and then politics.

As I approached the podium on the day I was nominated to be Speaker, someone said to me, "Your parents would be so proud." I thought, "I guess so, but my parents did not raise me to be Speaker of the House; they raised me to be holy."

"Holy" didn't mean kneeling down all the time and praying. It meant kindness toward others and again, as Speaker, policies that promote fairness and respect. I never thought about it in terms of my being in elected office.

My Catholicism has always been a source of strength for me. I pray a lot. I pray for my colleagues—Democrats and Republicans—and for my adversaries, because I want to be respectful of where they're coming from on issues, even though I don't think they're very charitable in some of their public policy.

I was a teenager when President Kennedy was running for office, and I witnessed the anti-Catholicism he faced. One of my inspirations is President Kennedy's speech in Texas when he spoke to a conference of Protestant ministers. He said:

> Because I am a Catholic, and no Catholic has ever been elected President, the real issues in this campaign have been obscured—perhaps deliberately . . . So it is apparently necessary for me to state once again—not what kind of church I believe in, for that should be important only to me—but what kind of America I believe in.

It was elevating. He suffered from anti-Catholicism, and because of him, other people didn't have to. A taboo was broken. I keep a picture of him in my office.

The priest in my church never denied Communion in our parish to pro-choice politicians. Some of my colleagues have felt that pain a lot more deeply, because in their dioceses and in their churches priests did deny pro-choice members the sacraments. I came from a Catholic family that wasn't pro-choice; they didn't share my view, but they respected it. They wished I wasn't so open about it. We were raised to believe that everyone had a free will and he or she was responsible for his or her own decisions. For me, that outlook was very consistent with women having the right to choose.

We go to church and we respect it for what it is to us. We don't make judgments about everything that it does. The pedophile scandal was a major sorrow for many of us, and I have some very strong views about the Church and how it dealt with that, but that was the *people* in the Church, as far as I'm concerned. *They* were not important enough to turn me away from the Church. Don't even let me go into Cardinal Law and that he has been rewarded with a princely title in Rome. It is just appalling. I cannot deal with that, so I don't. But I guess it's my family background of just saying, "You don't attack the

Church." That's just the way it is. It's too ingrained, and I'm too old. So you just go with what you believe, what the Church means to you. And these are *people*; they're not the rock on which the Church was built, that's for sure.

I think about heaven a good deal the older I get. Heaven is your reward for living a good life. That is to say, a good life is its own reward. I don't think we'll be floating around on clouds, but I do subscribe to "Pascal's Wager," which says that you might as well live a good life just in case there's something after. There could be something very spiritual that happens after death.

Hell is the absence of the spirituality of a good life. I don't think we're going to be fried on pitchforks.

I go to churches all over the country because I travel a great deal. In our cathedral in San Francisco the archbishop got a standing ovation when he spoke about eliminating all nuclear weapons from the face of the earth and stopping proliferation of weapons of mass destruction. In my church there's a focus on the alleviation of poverty and kindness toward others. In other churches throughout the country, you have the nonnegotiables—stem cell research, women's right to choose, cloning, euthanasia, and gay marriage. There's great time spent on those issues instead of on what is the fundamental principle of our faith: We're all part of the body of Christ and so therefore everyone is worthy of respect. We have a responsibility if people are poor or sick to help them. I gave myself this book for Christmas: *Thus Saith the Lord: The Revolutionary Moral Vision of Isaiah and Jeremiah* by Richard Rubenstein. The book discusses the tragedy of Hurricane Katrina:

> The consequences of corrupt, callous, and short-sighted government policies may not seem serious so long as their primary victims are poor and voiceless people. But those evils put the whole society at risk. Isaiah recognized that unjust government dissolves and demoralizes communities leaving them unprotected.

That passage is not unlike what Pope Benedict XVI has in his first encyclical, which was released in April 2006, called "God Is Love." In it he says, "Any government that is not formed to promote justice is just a bunch of thieves." Benedict was quoting Augustine, who said that sixteen centuries ago, and he was made a saint. He then went on to say, "Sometimes it's difficult to define justice but in doing so we must be aware of the danger of ethical blindness caused by the dazzling power of money and special interest." I quote that on the floor all the time. My colleagues are all used to it.

I feel very close to Christ. If that's separate from the Church, I don't know. What a remarkable and wonderful way to lead a life—to have Christ as your savior. When people look at me askance for my faith, I think, "I have a gift."

There were some moments I didn't feel separate from the Church, but I felt let down. In 1968 the pope issued the encyclical *Humanae Vitae* on human life. I was having my fourth child in four years. I thought that there might be some understanding by the Church. I had no complaint in terms of my own life—we could afford a big family and we had a loving situation—but there wasn't any understanding by the Church for people honoring their own sense of responsibility and what they could handle with dignity. I remember being so optimistic that this encyclical was coming. I couldn't wait until it came. I ran for the papers. It was such a letdown. It was one of those moments where you say, "I guess they've made their decision and the rest of us have to make ours." It was a missed opportunity for the Church.

I've always been pro-choice. To me, it's like saying, "Should we surrender our brains?" I feel very comfortable with it.

I'm constantly inspired by the work of Catholics in the community. In San Francisco Father Floyd Lotito has headed up St. Anthony's Dining Room, which has served thousands of meals to the needy for over forty years. I said to him one day, "Father, why is it that you don't burn out?" And he said, "My parents raised me to believe that God loved poor people in a very special way, and therefore we have to treat them in a very special way."

FRANK MCCOURT

*Francis "Frank" McCourt (b. August 19, 1930) is one of
the master storytellers of American literature. He received
the Pulitzer Prize for his memoir Angela's Ashes (1996),
which details his childhood as a poor Irish Catholic in
Limerick.*

    McCourt no longer follows the Catholic faith.

. . . .

Hell is a dark place. The temperature is about a million degrees, the walls are a million miles thick, and you're there for eternity. As little kids, we tried to wrap our minds over eternity, and the priests would say, "Imagine a bird goes to a mountain a million miles high and a million miles wide. Once every million years he takes a little grain of sand to another place. Then in a million years he comes back and takes another grain of sand. He's creating this mountain a million miles high and a million miles wide. Imagine the bird going back and forth creating this mountain; that's eternity." We could almost grasp that, the image of the mountain growing in a million years, but that would've been a very tired bird.

Every priest must have been trained in suffering and horror.

Heaven, on the other hand, is a milky place. God is sitting on his throne, and the Virgin Mary is to his right, St. Joseph and the archangels Michael and Gabriel are there, but there's nothing happening. We were told, "The rewards for leading a good and virtuous life are to stand before the throne of God gazing on his divine countenance in all wonder and reverence for all eternity," which sounds a bit like the bird.

Now I believe that when you die there's nothing—oblivion and memories.

If we could prove conclusively that your life ends with your last breath, it would change the whole course of history. Nobody would give a shit if there's no afterlife.

One day I piped up in class. We were preparing for confirmation and had gone through the seven deadly sins. There were times when I was nauseatingly goody-goody. So I said, "Sir, I know the first deadly sin." He said, "Oh, you do? What's the first deadly sin?" I said, "It's sloth." He said, "Is that right?" And I replied, "Yes, because if you commit sloth you're doing nothing, and if you're doing nothing you can't be committing the other deadly sins." That led to a thrashing around the room, for thinking.

You didn't ask questions in class, but we were little amateur theologians on the schoolyard.

We would talk about the Trinity and wonder what a virgin was. We were thirteen or fourteen when we discovered anything about sex, because anything to do with the flesh was the forbidden subject. My mother would never admit that anything natural happened; angels delivered us. We knew not to ask questions.

We had a very unhealthy relationship with girls. When I became a teacher, I saw the ease among boys and girls in high school. I envied them. When I did meet women, I didn't know what to say to them. I'd just like leaping on them. That's it. Sex. It took three marriages before I reached a plateau of health.

Pedophilia was common in Ireland. This priest came to our school and invited us to join the Holy Ghost Fathers as missionaries in Kenya. He said if anybody was interested he'd give us a private appointment. He said he had to examine me physically and that I had to lie in his lap and he would put his ear on my chest and his hands would wander. I said, "I have to leave."

I was eleven or twelve and ashamed. I knew it happened to other kids in the class. I didn't know how far he went with them and nobody was saying anything.

It was fear that made me leave, because I couldn't reconcile the collar with the groping hands. In Ireland they were sick; they went for boys. Maybe they thought the girls would spill the beans faster.

I still can't figure out faith, because I suppose I had it and then I realized I didn't have it; it was imposed on me.

I came to New York and started going about in a new way— Saturday night bars and Sunday morning I would be hung over, sleeping with a woman. I wouldn't go to Mass and the guilt accumulated.

It was also fear. What if I die tonight? I would go to hell. But it dissipates after a while.

I saw the antics of the Church and began to think more and more about the contradictions. I began to find a great lack of love and too much fear, in the Irish Catholic Church especially. It was inconsistent, because love is the central theme of Catholicism. I didn't find it, and I had to go another more human direction.

I feel more and more aware of the mystery, and I am reconciled to the oblivion that is coming. I see no proof of anything else, if it is a matter of faith. I admire people who have faith in God. It must be a great comfort to them, but I had to get out from under the fear and the guilt.

All the religions are laid out like a great buffet, and I take what I want from each of them. Buddhism is the only religion, as far as I know, that never started a war. All of the Buddhist priests committed in Vietnam—they immolated themselves.

Sometimes I wish I could go back into teaching and tell the kids what I've discovered since. I wasn't put on this earth to be Irish or Catholic or a Jew or a Protestant. I was put here naked and everything was injected into me.

Irish history was imposed on us. We were brainwashed and conditioned to believe that the English were villains, which they were to a certain extent. We never had teachers or priests who told us to think for ourselves. We were told what to think and how to feel. When I got older, I realized I had discarded what I didn't want.

If you steal from your mother's purse, if you utter a curse, you tell that to your priest and your soul is wiped clean. Anybody who is a Catholic knows this. When you go to confession as a teenager, you walk out of the church on air. Then you come over to America and people tell you to go to therapy. You just keep peeling the onion. It's a very witty vegetable. I'll put the onion on my tombstone.

When I wrote *Angela's Ashes*, I thought I wrote a very mild book. My brother said, "You pulled your punches." I could have gone deeper into it. You have to know you can go so far before people become disgusted. I could have, for instance, described the lavatory that was outside of our house, which was used by the whole lane. People would empty everything into this lavatory, and because of this I got typhoid fever. I could have gone into greater detail about the rats and vermin in there. I could have described what it was like in the morning getting up. You were cold, damp, and miserable. But you have to use your judgment.

I didn't think much about what I was revealing. I thought I revealed very little. Certain people who were the guardians of Limerick's virtue said I'd shamed the city.

My mother used to say, forget about Limerick, you're in America now. I couldn't forget. As a teacher, I saw things in my classroom. I saw kids who were subject to incestuous abuse by their fathers, kids who were hungry, and kids on drugs.

I think the one organization that kept us alive in Limerick was the St. Vincent de Paul Society. If this society had not existed, we would have had no place to go to get tea, bread, sugar, and flour. Our mother would have had to put us in an orphanage.

I don't remember a single priest in all of Limerick who had a sense of humor, and this is the race of people known for their "humane" side. They were afraid to let go, and we had to keep our mouths shut. We'd go outside and make fun of them. Otherwise, it was humorless. Our mimicry and mockery kept us going.

What you find in institutions is that there are jokes that mimic the sergeants; the officers; the whole bureaucracy in prisons, hospitals, and schools—kids are always mimicking. That's what keeps you going in these soulless organizations, and poverty is a kind of institution. You are down in some slum, and if you don't have a sense of humor, you don't last. Kids know when they have a sourpuss kid and that's the one they pick on.

Catholicism was, whatever it is, a rich experience. I'm glad that I've reached this stage of my life where I'm able to look back, not with anger, but with almost gratitude for the experiences I had. Maybe I was damaged by it for a long time—we all were—but I can make use of it and that's the gift. A lot of my contemporaries have been damaged badly. They would go off to England and become alcoholics; that was the outcome of our backdrop—the alcoholism and the despair.

FRANK BUTLER

Francis J. Butler (b. February 4, 1945) is president of Foundations and Donors Interested in Catholic Activities, Inc. (FADICA), a consortium of fifty private philanthropic entities. Butler has directed FADICA for over twenty-five years as the organization has played a proactive role in developing and forming a new generation of lay leaders for Catholic institutions.

. . . .

I'm from a big Irish Catholic family, one of six kids. I wanted very much to be a priest, so I went into the seminary and was there for nine years, until I decided that I wanted to be married. I left the seminary but then had a very strong pull, because of this experience, to stay in something related to religion or my faith. After I got my master's and then a doctorate in theology in 1972, I went to work for the Catholic hierarchy in the social justice office, mostly on Capitol Hill, on poverty and urban issues.

In 1980 I was asked by FADICA (Foundations and Donors Interested in Catholic Activities) to work with them. FADICA comprises the fifty largest Catholic foundations in the world, representing a billion dollars a year in giving, most of which has an impact on the Church worldwide. It was a wonderful opportunity to work with highly motivated people, and I've been with this organization for twenty-five years.

I could recite a lot of cases where we've hit home runs for the Catholic Church but where we started out with just enormous amounts of anger. Some years ago, we commissioned research on the unpaid retirement liability that Catholic sisters had because of their low-paid service to the Church. They'd worked basically for stipends for schools and were never able to set aside funds for their old age. The system of taking care of the sisters was beginning to fall apart, because nobody wanted to be a nun anymore. We moved the entire hierarchy to start a program nationally and over half a billion dollars has been raised so far; the public has been educated, so now they know that the religious aren't provided for in their retirement.

Still, today nuns are not usually provided for in retirement. But they are better able to determine how they would like to live out their lives without economic stress. We found sisters who were chambermaids in motels just to bring income into their convent. We had a convent in New York, a small group, that went out to a bank and borrowed to pay for the funeral of one of its members and it couldn't pay the loan back. There were these godawful stories all around, and the sisters blamed themselves. They were ashamed and didn't want to talk about it publicly, so it was a difficult issue to move on.

You can see a dramatic difference with the sisters who run the hospitals. The Catholic Church sponsors about a fifth of the hospital beds in the country, which is huge, and those sisters don't have a problem because the salaries in the hospitals are basically driven by Medicare. They are doing fine, but they are really the exception. Most sisters taught in schools or did social work, and they have nothing.

The situation in New Orleans is amazing; most of the religious women were really in terrible straits. The Church has raised about $180 million to rebuild the Church infrastructure, but all that is going through the diocesan systems and is not going to the religious. They can't get money from FEMA either, so they are just sort of stuck between a rock and a hard place, and their mother houses are wrecked. These older women, women over age seventy, are still trying to teach and serve the poor, but they can't get help, so we are organizing something right now.

Part of my work here is to turn all people with righteous anger in a constructive direction. I bridge the worlds of Church leadership and everyday Catholicism. I know how the institution of the Church is led and it isn't as bad as people sometimes think. It's an amazing institution and achieves enormous good in the world. But I understand the Church can be a sinful institution. It is made up of human beings, so you're going to get all kinds of behavior.

When I worked for the Conference of Bishops, I led a program called the Action Conference, which aimed to elicit social commentary, to take the theme of social justice and look at injustice in America. Cardinal John Dearden of Detroit, who chaired the Vatican II document to unleash this great potential of laypeople who'd been fairly passive in the Church, was our chairman.

We held hearings all around the country. People with brown lung disease from working in the textile mills, illegal aliens, American Indians, farmworkers in California, people from inner-city ghettos and rural hallows all testified. I saw real greatness in the hierarchy; I saw these bishops listening attentively to these people and their lives. We saw change occurring. They were getting it—this whole justice thing wasn't just poetry to them. Up until that time, I'm not sure a lot of bishops understood Catholic social teaching, but they began to understand through this listening process how injustice actually played out in people's lives. This process led to a major conference on justice in 1976. The conference was somewhat traumatic for the Church, because Church leaders heard more than they wanted to hear not only about injustice in society but also injustice inside the Church. Participants talked about the treatment of women by the Church, compensation of their own employees, racism and discrimination; in other words, the application of Catholic social teaching to its day-to-day practices. It took on a very controversial edge, and after the conference was over the whole hierarchy had a very difficult time reaching agreement about how to respond.

In the end, it turned out that much change did occur as a result of the whole process. Bishops moved forward with a stronger voice on justice and for the next several years employed a more pastoral, listening, consultative manner of working among their flock. It's a great way to lead the Church, because God makes his presence known not just through scripture and tradition and not just to clergy and Catholics but through everyone. And it's through the experience of people that we can come to know what God is saying about our world.

Catholic social justice is the essential part of the Gospel itself, and you can't be a Catholic and opt out of that. All can share in God's blessings. If you look at the Protestant tradition, it's very much focused on the individual. Ours is a little more horizontal: You get your salvation in the Catholic faith because of your linkage to the faith community. In a way, you could say that you're not going to get to heaven by your own individual efforts but by Christ's, and that's why you must stay connected to his body, the Church community. That is why when you are excommunicated people say you are dead, you're not going to make it, and you are out of the Christian community. The Christian community is Christ.

God is in each of our lives and guides our lives. I know that God works through me, it doesn't have anything to do with wearing a Roman collar or not. He is here! We have to figure out a process where the people of God can somehow share their experience of God so the whole community is enriched. Each one of us has a vocation, a calling by God for the community; it is a gift for the community. It is not for ourselves but for the others. In everyday Catholicism we don't have a process to allow this reality to come forth and influence the Church's life so we waste all of this potential that we have. We have low participation, and we often are more concerned about excluding people rather than including people.

I love the baptism of Jesus in the Jordan. Jesus goes down into the water and when he comes out he hears the voice, "This is my beloved son." We're all beloved daughters and beloved sons; we're Christ in the world. This was the scene that marked Jesus' first public ministry. That is my favorite passage; it speaks to me the most, because I like to think of my life and mission in that way. I'm loved in my identity, which has nothing to do with titles. It has nothing to do with what I own, how many kids I have, what status I have, nothing! My identity is linked to that relationship with my heavenly Father as Jesus' was. I think that is the security that every Christian has to dwell on, and we don't appreciate it. It's all about finding God in yourself and others around you; that is the core thing. I also love the prodigal son story. That is my image of the Father, welcoming me in, throwing a party. Forget the past and welcome back.

When I pray, I like to be with a lot of people. Focus on the fact that Christ is present, because we're all there. I like a good liturgy, good music, and to be surrounded by my friends, focused on the Lord. I can also appreciate the older liturgy with lots of smoke, mystery, and darkness. My sense is that the Holy Spirit is inside each one of us and constantly praying for us. What we do in prayer is tap into that action; it's going on constantly throughout the day.

If I were pope, I'd make no statements for a year, no pronouncements at all. I think the Church does better to listen than to speak. There is not enough observing of where God is in the world by the Church, and it is transformative for people to listen. So I would like to see the Church quiet down. I'd try to get rid of the fear and the anger. I think those are the two things that are driving the Church in the wrong direction. Jesus said that fear is useless. I don't know if we appreciate as Catholics that we need more faith that we're not alone and more confidence that the example of well-lived, loving, and just lives will do more to change the world than just words.

Bishops are fine and some are heroic too, but they aren't the whole Church. Let's embrace and empower everybody to talk about how God works in their lives. We have to ask ourselves, where would Jesus be today? He'd be with all the folks who are out in the margins, people who feel rejected, pulling them all in; that is the kind of Church we want.

The danger is that Church leaders can make religion a burden rather than a liberation from the burdens of human existence, and again, we go back to the master on this. He did not have good things to say to those who were making religion difficult.

I gave a talk at Boston College on a code of professional ethics in the Church. I said, "If you're a Church leader you should give part of your time in direct service to the poor." I think we'd hear fewer pronouncements if the bishops were actually out there, knew the poor directly, served people, and saw how difficult this life is. I think their sense of compassion would grow and that is what is missing. Jesus was the compassion of God, and these leaders have to understand that life is difficult for everybody of all classes; it's most particularly difficult for the poor. When you see that, you'll be less judgmental, more open, more loving, and that is what we need in leaders: We need them to love people.

GABRIEL BYRNE

Gabriel Byrne (b. May 12, 1950) is an acclaimed actor, writer, producer, and social justice activist. His extensive filmography includes The Usual Suspects, Little Women, Ghost Ship, Spider, Vanity Fair, The Bridge of San Luis Rey, *and* Emotional Arithmetic.

Byrne is no longer a practicing Catholic.

. . . .

I have a very conflicted attitude about the Church. I come from a background where people believe that having a priest in the family is the greatest blessing God can bestow. It's an Irish badge of honor. The Irish had supplied Africa and the Far East with so many missionaries. At church there was a little collection box for the missionaries in Africa, with a little black boy, and you put in a coin and he'd nod his head in thanks. One never knew where that money was going and why it was being collected, but we just assumed, like everything else, it was the right thing to do.

My faith at that time was the faith of a child, which doesn't have logic. I don't know if logic and faith are actually compatible. To have faith you have to—in a way—deny logic. I think my faith was mixed up with a notion of home and security. I didn't have a very stable home life, so the Church provided me with that. All the questions that I had were answered there. And I didn't have to ask many complicated questions of myself or the world around me. If I suffered in this world, I'd go to heaven. If I did this, it was a sin—things were very clear-cut. I went away at twelve to be a priest and I left the seminary when I was seventeen. I'm no longer a practicing Catholic. I don't practice any form of institutionalized religion.

Looking back, I recognize joining the seminary was part of a desire to escape from the world, a world that some days seemed unbearable. It was a shelter from the storm, a very seductive idea. I didn't realize how much the theatre and the Church influence each other and how close they are in terms of what they provide to people.

I went to church the other day in Brooklyn, not expecting to feel anything, but I've always gone in to church to sit for a few minutes and try to connect with something greater than myself. I realized that the Church captures silence brilliantly. Most churches enshrine or encapsulate the silence. Silence forces you to come into contact with yourself. You can be walking on the street and thinking, but there is nothing quite like suddenly being in a hushed, silent building. The Church understood, and still does, the power of silence. If you look at the architectural mechanics of the Church, it's just like the theater—you have the seats, the audience, the stage, the main actors, the theatrical effects like the candles, the flowers, and you have the incense.

There is a lot of pageantry and a lot of the deep understanding of the effect on the deepest emotions. Some say the light from the stained glass produces an effect that is extremely calming and uplifting. Incense inhaled produces a feeling of relaxation. Candlelight brings everything into dramatic relief. These things are not accidents, so the connection between the theater and church is to me very obvious and very powerful.

Faith to me is a decision to believe despite evidence to the contrary; it's a brave thing to do. One becomes an active participant in the world when he or she believes in something. Faith, optimism, and hope—we have to have those things as human beings; otherwise, life makes no sense whatsoever. Life is unbearable because there is nothing that we can see beyond ourselves. On the other hand, I do understand that realistic view of the world, the rejection of faith, the rejection of God. There are people who see faith and religious exercise as being merely the mechanics of following a huge fairy tale and that actually there is nothing after this. There is nothing really before this; there just is what there is.

I suffered in my early childhood and in my adolescence at the hands of people who aren't equipped to be representatives of the ideal of Christianity.

I don't believe that celibacy contributes any more to the well-being of the Catholic Church. And I don't think Christ came down to earth to say that man should be celibate. Actually, the Church hierarchy introduced celibacy as a purely utilitarian function so that they wouldn't have to pay the dependents of the priests who got women pregnant. They invented a notion of celibacy, which I regard as a sin against human life, because it denies the one thing that is God given—the need, the blessed urge, to procreate life. To deny that is to deny the humanity of people, and to institutionalize celibacy makes the sin even greater.

The Episcopalian, the Protestant, and the Anglican religions all survive with man being married, and there is absolutely nothing wrong with a woman being involved in the life of a man whose job it is to be the pastor of his flock. As a result of that denial of the human urge to procreate and have a loving relationship with another human being, you pervert that instinct and a lot of people who are in the Church in positions of responsibility and power become debased and affected in a negative way.

Where does their sexual urge go? You put a man in charge of forty boys and it's actually OK for him to be sexually free with the young boys and not OK for him to be with a woman. As long as celibacy survives, people will be drawn to the priesthood for all the wrong reasons. People who are totally unsuited to the priesthood enter into it. They're institutionalized, and as a result, people like me suffer.

I was sexually abused.

I wrote about what happened in a magazine in Ireland some years ago. Actually, it was a letter of forgiveness to this man who'd abused me. Nobody mentioned the article—ever. They didn't come up and say, "It happened to me, too," "Thanks for saying this," or "I know what you went through." I think there is a certain amount of shame in it and people think, let's just ignore it. So—after I'd written the piece—I was left with the feeling that I'd stood up in front of the class, said what'd happened to me, and that I was greeted with total silence and then told to sit down. Then, of course, you feel another sense of, Maybe I shouldn't have said that or written that.

The letter was an attempt to try to find the humanity of the man and to try to understand the world that'd created him by celibacy, by him being institutionalized, by the silence code of the Church and the way they treated it. It was an attempt to understand that world and my place as an innocent kid in it. Was he really to blame or was the Church and the society that produced him to blame as well?

I hadn't thought of it for a long time. Then one day I met him at a football match, and he recognized me from films and said hello. I looked at him; he didn't know that I knew him or what I knew about him. He didn't make that connection, but I, of course, did.

He was a man who was obviously used to living alone with hair grown over his ears—an uncared-for man in a beret shouting at the football field the things that he used to shout at us. "Harder! Drive it! Drive it!" I tracked him down to this nursing home, and I called him and asked if he remembered me. He asked me what my name was and said, "No, I don't remember anybody with that name." And then, at the end of a long pause, he said, "Did you use to sit in the front row?" I said, "Yes. I was really good at Latin. You used to call me G—that was your nickname for me."

I told him I was really good in Latin because I wanted him to think I was a really good student; I liked that he liked me. He gave me encouragement. He was nice to me, and then he repeated, "What is your name?" I told him my name again, and he said that it couldn't be true, because he only knows one man with that name and he's a film star. I said, "That is me," and there was another long silence and he said, "I'm talking to Gabriel Byrne, the film star? Why did you call on me?" I couldn't say anything. I really could not say what I had to say.

What I remembered more than anything else was that he had a very kind voice, a very gentle voice, and as a young kid who lived in an unstable background, an older person with a very kind voice was shelter from the storm. Here I was after all these years and there was still a part of me saying, this man has a gentle voice. I thought I'd be angry; I thought I'd be upset, but I wasn't. I just asked myself, where'd my anger go, where'd my hurt and disappointment go? I know where it went. It went deep inside me, and yet I couldn't confront him. I later heard he died in his sleep.

It makes you think about life, that somebody who really deserves life dies in great pain and somebody who deserves to die in great pain goes in their sleep. What's God's purpose in that? People abuse; they don't get caught. They die quietly. People do incredibly great things for people and they die violently. There is no justice. It's kind of a myth to believe that the universe is somehow a place of order—that if you do this, then that'll happen.

I've tried to forgive him. That piece I wrote is because, deep, deep, deep down, I feel that I've forgiven. I probably haven't, but the nature of forgiveness is that you have to take the action to forgive and ultimately one hopes that real forgiveness will come from it. I saw him as a man trapped by ignorance, the institution, bigger players, and his family—a man who should've been married or a man who should've been gay. He shouldn't have been in a room living by himself or with other men teaching kids.

I remember, at five years of age, being told that if I did something wrong, which could've been as banal as eating sweets before dinner, I'd burn in hell physically for eternity. At that age, to be thinking that if you did something bad you'd burn in hell—forget about enjoying life as a kid. Take your five-year-old head and try to understand the notion of eternity.

I remember a nun in front of the classroom striking a match and putting the match to her finger. We were all dumbstruck; we were six or seven at that time and she said, "My finger is like your soul, and the flame is like the flames of hell, and that is how your soul burns for all time."

There is a huge difference between that kind of perverted Catholicism and the ideas of Christianity. I'm not passing on Catholicism to my kids. I'm not passing on any form of institutionalized religion. I think that the world of religion and the world of spirituality are two different things. What I pass on to them, I hope, is what I believe to be the crux of Christianity, which is love thy neighbor as thyself. Contained in that is a recipe for some kind of definition of happiness. What my Catholicism taught me was to deny who I was, to denigrate it, to be ashamed of it, to not acknowledge it, and to not love myself.

The Catholic Church has been guilty of not loving other people, and when church and state get into bed together and the ideals of Christianity are used in pursuit of the political, monetary, and worldly ends, that is a denial of Christianity. I believe in the principles of Christianity but also in the principles of Judaism and they contain the same message. I don't believe in an afterlife. I don't believe in a God. I don't believe that we live in a world of order. I believe we live in a world of chaos and the institutions we've brought to bear to prevent that chaos from becoming all enveloping are law, religion, and education. They give you an illusion that you can control chaos, but actually every single day there are instances that chaos is the norm and not order. I don't believe that there is necessarily a cosmic consequence to action.

Paris and Rome are built on violence and blood; at the heart of beauty is something dark. Yeats said it, which is a great line: "A pity beyond all telling is hid in the heart of love." So true, you cannot love without the knowledge of loss. When I think of spirituality I think of the things of the spirit; I believe in the spirit of a human being, I believe in good spirits—the soul (for want of a better description) of a human being. Faith is a very personal decision. I envy people who have it. It may be our only purpose that we don't know; not knowing might be the only thing that makes sense in this world. When you look at what you do for a living, you have to say, this is what I do, how can I use what I do in some way not to change the world, but at least to raise awareness?

Susan Sarandon

Susan Sarandon (b. October 4, 1946) is an Academy Award–winning American actress. Her movies include Dead Man Walking, *for which she won the Academy Award (1995),* Stepmom *(1998),* Anywhere but Here *(1999),* Cradle Will Rock *(1999),* Shall We Dance? *(2004),* Alfie *(2004),* Elizabethtown *(2005), and* Enchanted *(2007).*

Throughout her career, Sarandon has promoted progressive causes, including gay, transgender, and transsexual rights; peace in Vietnam, Central America, and Iraq; gun control; the environment; women's rights; and a host of other human rights issues.

. . . .

I was born in New York City and raised in Jackson Heights until it
was no longer economically feasible. Then we moved to New Jersey and were in this community where everybody had a huge number of children. I think there were maybe twenty families that
populated the entire grammar school. Some families had eighteen
kids. We had nine, all baptized.

I was told very early on by the nuns that I had an "overabundance of original sin." I was a quiet kid, but I was curious. I asked
the wrong questions. And the first brush I had that led to this diag-
nosis of an overabundance of original sin came when I was in third
grade and they were talking about how you're only really married if
you're married in the Catholic Church. I asked, "Then how were
Joseph and Mary married if Jesus didn't invent it until later?" That
gave me a place in the hallway.

I went to church every afternoon. The boys were separated from
the girls in this school. You could look longingly at them across the
asphalt parking lot, which they used as the playground, but nobody
talked. From the second grade on, they separated you according to
gender.

I was Mary in the school play, and on my lunch hour I would go
to the church. When the other girls were meeting the boys and making out in the confessionals, I was praying to have the strength not
to deny my faith when the communists came to hang us upside down
on crosses.

I took it very seriously. I wanted to be a good person. I took my
rosary beads to bed with me at night until one night, when I was
seven or eight, I looked down and they were glowing, and I thought,
"Oh my God, I'm about to have a vision. The Blessed Virgin is about
to come in the door." And I realized I didn't want her to come. I was

terrified. That's when I realized maybe I wasn't the Catholic girl I thought I was. Of course my aunt had given me these glow-in-the-dark beads and hadn't told me as much.

But I didn't "get" the exclusivity of the Catholic Church or the joylessness of a lot of the nuns. I thought, in the beginning, that there were boys and girls and nuns, three genders because the nuns had male names and mustaches. I heard they had shaved heads. So I was very confused in the beginning. Did they sleep in black nightgowns?

I did have a fabulous nun, Sister Margo, who was very young. I was in love with her. Compared with everybody else I was experiencing, she was like a gift. And she stayed in the order.

I was the only one in my family who didn't go to a Catholic high school, and to this day this is given as an explanation of what went wrong with me. I was in accelerated classes with almost all Jewish kids who were not the least bit apologetic for killing Christ. I was stunned. This was my first brush with anything outside—any kind of heartfelt religion that wasn't Catholic. We still continued every Sunday to go to church.

I ended up at the Catholic University of America in Washington, D.C., when all hell was breaking loose. It was 1965, so there were assassinations, the city was burning, and all the nuns and priests were leaving and running away with each other. I was working in the drama department, on the switchboard, because I needed money to go to school. The guy who was in the office with me was this fabulous man who was clearly gay, and I remember when *The Boys in the Band* came out. It was written by somebody who went to Catholic University and the powers that be insisted it was a musical. They weren't dealing with the homosexuality aspect of it at all.

The easiest way to a crisis of faith is to actually study the Catholic Church, to understand the gestation of the Church and the politicizing of Christ's words—how in Italy you became a cardinal as part of a land grant. Going back even further, you realize who wrote what and what they left out. I started to question blind faith and got really angry at the way Christ's life had been manipulated, used, and

was continuing to be used—the exclusion of women and the imprac-
ticality of it. That kind of did it for organized religion as far as I was
concerned.

My kids are baptized, because why not give them that? I was living in Rome with my daughter, and I wasn't married to her father. So
I thought, "Well, let's have a baptism—it gives the family something." But it wasn't because I was taking away the original sin from
her. I really don't believe that. I think God, whatever God is, is much
bigger than all these little read-the-fine-print kind of things. I think
God doesn't mind if you're gay. I don't think God minds if you're
not married if you're committed to each other, if you are kind.

I'm a spiritual person, but in college I started to resent institutionalized religion. You look around now and where are the spiritual
leaders of the Catholic Church about Iraq, for instance? If you go to
third-world countries, if you go to South America and Central America, which I did do, then you see priests and nuns who are putting
their lives on the line to help the poor, to find them education, to
free them from injustice, and for me that's what the Church should
be. That's what the Church here wasn't. Certainly you can find religious people who understand that once you open that door and you
start to educate yourself about injustice, you have a responsibility.

It's probably not a coincidence that I named my daughter after
Eve. Eve was the first person who thought for herself. I resent that
the Church tries to instill in people that whole "if you eat of the tree
of knowledge, if you want to know, you'll be out on your butt and
you'll be shamed into having to be a farmer and the Father won't
take care of you." I resent it when the government does that, too. I
think you have a responsibility toward yourself and other people to be
informed. And I think the real words of Christ, and of all the leaders
who were Christlike in all the various religions, say that you have a
responsibility to your fellow man, and we've lost that. We've lost the
essence of that spirituality, and so I resented the Church that did
that and that also relegated women to a lower status. Even now, nuns
are at the bottom of the food chain. If they start to ask questions, an

order is slapped on them to be quiet. Not being a real spiritual leader is what's going to kill the Church. It's atrophying.

I know there are some Catholic schools that are teaching social justice but it wasn't my experience. It was all about what you couldn't do. It was joyless. So when I found the book *Dead Man Walking*, here was a nun, Sister Helen Prejean, who was finding a way to stay in the Church but at the same time was so remarkable, so religious, funny, joyful, and celebratory. She started off as a cloister and, eventually, in working with the poor, became completely politicized. You can't work with the poor and not become politicized.

Sister Helen brought Pope John Paul a copy of *Dead Man Walking* and when she showed him how some of his words were being twisted to support the death penalty, he issued a statement that was more specifically against capital punishment. We've failed to make education, the poor, and the environment moral issues from a Catholic perspective.

In *Dead Man Walking*, I was playing a specific person who enlightened me because she had found some way to stay in the Church and believe in the Church and yet she was doing the things she was doing. When I met her, she was just Sister Helen. I don't know if it's her accent or the way she talks, but she gives the impression that she's still finding her way. She tells you things that have happened but there's this way that she talks that involves you in the process, as if it's still open-ended. She doesn't speak down to you. She still has that little bit of wonder that's going on when she's just come out of another death row experience—"And Susan, I'm telling you I saw the face." She brings you on her journey. She's a laugher and an eater. She's joyful, and she sings.

I knew her for more than a year. She was part of our family before Tim [Tim Robbins, who directed and produced *Dead Man Walking*, is the longtime partner of Susan Sarandon] even decided to do it.

The institution of the Church is so rigid, so old-fashioned, and so ignorant in terms of how it's dealing with people, that it's really shooting itself in the foot. I was very moved by Sister Helen and her faith. She's continued to talk to us and pointed us in the direction of Gnostic gospels.

I used to love going to the Mass in Latin. I loved the incense. I loved the whole spectacle of it. It was one of the saddest things to me when everyone started singing folk songs in English and shaking hands. I really loved the ceremonies of the Church. I loved reading about the saints. Now I look back on them and they all seem like they had eating disorders and were completely masochistic—these gals who were doing all this weird stuff to themselves. These were lives we were supposed to emulate. It sets up a glorified victim—women celebrated because they've suffered and sacrificed.

I talk to God. I talk to Her. I'm grateful for my life. The thing that I love about Jesus was that he talked about the divine in everyone. Through time, the priests have really escalated and enhanced your dependency upon them to interpret what's going on. Originally, they were not designed to be the gateway to your redemption but as time went on, the Church glorified your need for them. What I relate to is the way Jesus lived his life, what he said, the divine in each of us, and the reverence for life, a life lived in peace.

Spirituality is innate. You can't have experienced birth, you can't have lived in the world, without seeing there's something bigger than you are. Is there some sort of specific deity that I go to pray to when I want something? No. There's somebody who I go to every day and I say thank you for my life. But I think it's that the holy is in every person. That's where everything belongs. I'm moved and awed when I meet people like Sister Helen; that to me reinforces spirituality. When you see your first dead person that you know and you see that they're no longer there, you realize how much of the spiritual makes a person who they are.

When I saw my kids upon their births, I thought they didn't look familiar. They're not a "mini-me." They're so completely who they are. I was so impressed by how strong their personalities and their presences were. They were like little aliens that had been plopped down. That was a huge wake-up call for me. Yet I know that my kids and I are connected in a way that leads me to believe that this is not the first time. So is that spirituality? I don't know if it's reincarnation.

Sometimes, I'm able to just stop and be present in my life. I look at the day and think about how lucky I am that I'm healthy. I'm at the age now where people even younger than I am have been struggling with cancer or depression. I'm lucky because in the business I'm in, what you have to keep trying to do is to suspend your expectation and be present in your life. When you're working, if you're an actor, it's about imagination, which leads to empathy, which leads to action—that's activism right there. The other half of it's that you have to be present.

We're lulled into being on this train that we're on, when we have all the things we have to accomplish throughout our day. You become a parent instead of a partner. You become a mother instead of a person with your children, because you have to function. Those definitions make you function, especially if you want to be a good parent. You're almost better off if you're a bad parent. Maybe your kids end up better off if you're not constantly all over them. Can you forgive yourself for not having the perfect house? Where do you find the time to stop nagging and sit and watch some stupid TV thing with your kids? You have to remind yourself to find those places where you connect with the people you love. You have to remind yourself to have lunch with your girlfriends. You have to remind yourself to breathe. It's a constant battle for me.

I don't know that there's a heaven. And there certainly isn't a hell. God is much bigger than that. I don't think God is really insulted if you take Her name in vain. God minds when you're cruel, when you lie, when you murder, and when you steal. And I think She wants you to take a day off. But I don't think She really cares if you get married or not or if you're gay. She wants to see people being kind to each other and respecting each other. A lot of these concepts are just inventions to comfort people, threaten people, and manipulate people.

If I were pope for a year, I'd sell off most of that stuff that's in the Vatican and eradicate poverty and disease. I'd try to find ways to bring hope to the world, try, in some way, to eliminate this huge gap between the rich and poor countries and rich and poor within countries. I think that would do a lot to encourage peace. It's difficult for people to think about peaceful solutions when they're suffering and have no future. It'd be impossible to convince one of my kids to strap explosives on their bodies, because they have hope in the future.

I'd definitely come out stronger against the death penalty. I'd really make it difficult.

I'd ask all the Catholics to be up in arms about an illegal war and to pay more attention to these people who are coming home—our young sons and daughters who are coming home mentally and physically maimed. And to go out from the churches instead of sitting there communicating with God, to go out and communicate with God by doing something.

GRACE WRIGHT

Grace Wright (b. June 3, 1964) ministers to the sick in St. Francis Xavier parish of Wilmette, Illinois, and is trained in Reiki therapy and Catholic healing practices. She's currently a part-time illustrator and graphic artist.

. . . .

A few years ago, I trained to become a minister of CARE, a person who has the ability to go the tabernacle after the host has been consecrated and take it out of the church to somebody in need. It's a privilege to be able to take the living Jesus with you, after you leave the church. The training is rigorous so that when you deliver Communion to somebody who is homebound, possibly psychologically needy, but still Catholic, who wants to receive Jesus, you won't go in and become a psychologist. You won't go in and try to cure them mentally and physically, but instead you'll be there to listen and help to bring the Holy Spirit to them.

The training ended with hands-on healing. It's about bringing energy to a person through the Holy Spirit. We used Reiki.

Right after the Reiki training, I was diagnosed with a brain tumor. It's going to be fine, but it was such a blessing that I had those healing people in my life at a time when it was scary.

Every time I have an opportunity to be a healing minister, it heals me; I get strength from it. I do believe it was God's hand that brought me to that situation.

Because a lot of people who are homebound are two generations ahead of me or even three, often the questions they have about the Gospel are things that I take for granted. For instance, there is this one woman, who just lost her dear friend, who was Jewish. She said to me, "I am concerned that Eliza is not in heaven because she is Jewish." My role is not to change her faith or our faith, but my role is to give her my impression of faith and also to help her through the thinking. I told her that I couldn't believe in a God that wouldn't allow everybody to enter heaven, especially the good, caring woman that she described Eliza to be. I believe that all people of all faiths will go to God. She was so relieved. And to think that it was such a simple gesture. Something that I wouldn't have given a second thought to really terrified her.

Healing happens in that way too. It was simply the healing of the mind in this instance. So I read the Gospel, talk a little bit, pray the Our Father, deliver the host, usually say a healing prayer, and then ask her if I can lay my hands on her or hold her hand or shoulder. Everyone usually says yes. You can feel the Holy Spirit just because of the one-on-one situation—being there, reaching out and touching a person not only physically but emotionally. That is what a healing minister is meant to do.

I feel the Holy Spirit working through me. I have such a strong faith. You get the person to totally relax. Something happens, and I certainly have a sensation, and sometimes a lack of strength, when I'm finished.

R. SCOTT APPLEBY

Scott Appleby (b. December 3, 1956) is a professor of history at the University of Notre Dame, where he also serves as the John M. Regan Jr. director of the Joan B. Kroc Institute for International Peace Studies. A historian of religion, he's a specialist on global fundamentalism and the author and editor of numerous books on Catholicism.

· ·

At the height of the sexual abuse crisis, Peggy Steinfels and I were the first laypeople, I think, ever to publicly address the U.S. Conference of Catholic Bishops—and we may be the last. It was a controversial thing to do, to give lay Catholics a voice before the bishops, and they wouldn't have done so if there hadn't been so much pressure and attention. It was important that we were allowed to speak.

Catholics were stunned and elated that the bishops allowed laity to speak their minds to them.

Peggy said, "This is how pathetic it is—we have no voice; you don't consult us; the only time we even get a chance to speak is in this low moment of crisis when you're almost compelled to listen to us, and we're not even sure you're going to listen to us." Her message was unmistakable.

I said that the bishops didn't "get" the sex abuse crisis; they didn't seem to understand the traumatic impact of a priest who consecrates the Eucharist, using the same hands to violate a child. The bishops' failure to acknowledge the suffering early on in the crisis, to indicate that they had a sense of the depth of the trauma, reinforced the unfortunate impression that they're out of touch with common human experience and insulated from everyday life. The scandal of the transfer of abusive priests back into settings where children and young adults were within their reach was bad enough. But the bishops compounded that failure by their clumsy pastoral response, or lack of response, to the victims. One would expect more compassionate and genuine concern from ordinary Christians, not to mention bishops.

One theme I touched on was the need for accountability within the Church, particularly among the bishops themselves. They didn't share what they were each doing in their respective dioceses with respect to handling the crisis. There was no uniformity in their pastoral or administrative practices because each bishop is independent, sovereign in his diocese, answerable ultimately only to the pope. The Vatican under John Paul II and Cardinal Ratzinger weakened any momentum toward empowering national conferences of bishops with genuine governing authority. And there are some bishops who prefer to be on their own in their diocese and not be governed by the consensus of the other U.S. bishops or be accountable to that consensus.

On this point, I suggested to the bishops, "Why don't you formulate and fully enforce national church policy on nondoctrinal matters that'd fit the U.S. legal, cultural, and political context? Rome is going to react the way it's going to react. What are you afraid of? You're bishops of the Church, successors to the apostles. You, as bishops, as cardinals, seem unable to stand up for yourselves and make autonomous decisions without having to run to Rome for endorsement of every decision. You know the American scene better than the Vatican; your judgments should be trusted."

The lack of accountability to other bishops encourages aloofness, not collegiality; it can make individual bishops isolated and insulated. To make matters worse, there is a clerical culture that distances some bishops and priests from the laity—the cultivation of a special club of the ordained, which at times has been quite authoritarian and even dismissive of the laity.

In a way, the crisis over the birth control decision, which continues today (although most laity practice artificial birth control), is another expression of lack of accountability in the Church. In an actual family, people must be accountable to one another; they must listen and adjust to the needs and experiences of the other. They must mutually discern the way forward. The magisterium's rejection of the testimony of laity as to their own experience of sexuality, raising children, and Christian family life flies in the face of mutual respect. It follows a model of divine revelation that sees all truth as being delivered only through the pope and bishops; but this wasn't the way the apostolic tradition of Catholic Christianity developed historically.

The culture of clericalism, of elevating the ordained priesthood, in particular the bishops, to a pedestal aloof from the laity, is in no way related to the Gospel but instead to power and to careerism within the Church.

John Paul II really turned the clock back in terms of clericalism. It was striking that he said very early in his pontificate to some newly ordained priests, "You're in the world but not of the world," which is the kind of language used before Vatican II, calling priests to be set apart from the laity. The positive side of this is, yes, priests have a particular call to holiness, but to set them apart from the laity, as above the laity, implies that they, and perhaps they alone, are the real Christians. That kind of Church-versus-the-world dualism was rejected by Vatican II, and laity just won't stand for it anymore.

The reaction of some of the men who've been appointed as bishops over the last twenty to thirty years has been "Good. Let's get rid of the rabble-rousers. We'll prune the Church, make it 'pure,'" which means, great, if you don't agree with us, you're out.

Many priests and bishops have the appropriate servant mentality. They interact openly with the laity, recognize their gifts, and do not stand on authority or expect special treatment. John Paul II was a great pope, but some of the younger priests who attempt to imitate him have veered away from the collegial model I've just described. Some of these cassock-wearing young Turks have an unfortunate tendency to think themselves vastly superior to, say, the woman in the parish who has directed the religious education program effectively, or the older priest who knows his people and how to serve them far better than the newly arrived, by-the-book "John Paul II priest." We can't afford as a Church to limit the talent pool to celibate males and relegate talented women and men to subordinate positions. It's institutional insanity.

A significant part of my research has been focused on the fact that the world's major religions are grappling with the same basic problem. How can we remain believers, in a world that is becoming increasingly secular and that seems to marginalize religion?

In the Fundamentalism Project we identified five ideological characteristics of fundamentalism and the first is reactivity to the marginalization of religion. These groups within Judaism, Christianity, Islam, and even Hinduism are reacting against specific threats. In Egypt the Muslim brotherhood reacted against Western oil and business "colonizing" the Middle East and bringing alcohol and prostitution and gambling. In Iran they react to this cultural colonialism as well. The most popular television show during the Iranian revolution was *Dallas*! The Western media are an insidious enemy, creeping along air waves across the border, offering a new, seductive way of life. Drugs, decadency, divorce, family breakdown—to those who would be called fundamentalists, this was all part of an atheist conspiracy. The fundamentalists tend to see the spread of Western lifestyles as not accidental but a unified historical force—a force that is demonic, undermining the foundation of family life, of ethics, and of virtue. They're reacting against what they see as the root cause of many of the social problems of our era.

The second characteristic of fundamentalists is selectivity. They are neither traditional religious nor uncritically modern people. They'll select certain ideas and instruments of science and technology in order to build their own alternative to the secular modern project. They're competitive; they want to build their own societies. They don't want those societies to be primitive or lacking science or technology, but they want them to be inspired by godliness.

The next trait is absolutism—the conviction that our sacred text, our traditions, and our knowledge of religion are absolutely true and superior to all other truths. We're not going to compromise with them, which is what the modern world does. Catholicism's proclamation of papal infallibility was a fundamentalist moment. A pope speaks without error. The biblical inerrancy taught by Protestant fundamentalists arose roughly at the same time, in the late nineteenth century. According to this doctrine, the Bible is free from any kind of error: It is completely accurate in its history, biology, and so on, as well as its theology. Nonetheless, fundamentalists do interpret these texts; it is impossible not to do so.

The fourth trait is dualism—that is, seeing the world as divided neatly between the elect and the reprobate, the children of light and the children of darkness. There's a cosmic war going on for the human soul, and one isn't neutral in such a war. You're one of us or one of them.

The fifth and most important characteristic of fundamentalism is millennialism. The term refers in its precise meaning to the Christian expectation of a thousand-year reign of Christ at the end of days. More broadly, when applied beyond evangelical Christianity, it refers to a general expectation of a dramatic, and often violent, turning point in history during which the true believers—that is, the fundamentalists—will exact their revenge on the infidel or lapsed. Interestingly, one finds in Sikhism, Buddhism, Hinduism, Judaism, Islam, Christianity, in all these scriptures and traditions, what I call "emergency clauses." They say, when the darkness comes, when the apocalyptic moment comes, all bets are off. Violence, normally prohibited, is now permitted; this is an emergency.

So 9/11 was not about the United States alone. It was played out on a larger imaginative canvas envisioning a long-term cosmic war. The immediate tactical audience of bin Laden was Muslim fence-sitters in Pakistan, Saudi Arabia, and across the Muslim world. Join us in the final battle against the infidels! Certainly we were the target of the planes, and they'd love to topple the U.S. government. But there is time to do that later. The first step is to awaken a billion Muslims who have thus far refused to commit violence in defense of Islam.

The Gospel of Luke has always been very important to me because it's about God's agency in siding with and caring for the poor, the underdog, the marginalized. Luke's heroine is the pregnant teenager, Mary. The Magnificat is a wonderful prayer. I love the line "He has confused the proud in their innermost thoughts." The incarnate son of God is born in a stable among animals; it's hard to miss the point about the dignity of humanity and the compassion of divinity.

I also love the parable where the paralytic is lowered from the roof and Jesus turns and says, "Your sins are forgiven." Then Jesus turns away and goes on with his business. Of course the poor fellow is happy to have his sins forgiven, but he'd like to walk. And so Jesus heals him. The important thing is that the sinner is now reconciled to the community. Luke teaches us that if we can be humble and rest in our need for others, if we can avoid the sin of pride that bedevils the Pharisees, we can live the eternal life of the Trinity.

The poor are God's people in this special way. It's not because God plays favorites; it's because the poor have no choice but to depend on others; they're more open to mutuality because they're so obviously needy. The rich have all kinds of ploys to avoid intimacy and real sharing but the heroine of Luke's Gospel is a young woman pregnant out of wedlock, doomed to be abandoned, who says yes to a command from God to enter into a life of heartache, compassion, suffering, freedom, love—all embodied in the Christ child she's bearing. "OK, if I must, *yes* to this."

I take great comfort and courage from her yes.

DAN McNEVIN

Dan McNevin (b. March 23, 1959) is a Stanford graduate and partner in a San Francisco real estate investment firm. As an area leader and media spokesperson for SNAP (Survivors Network of those Abused by Priests)—from 2003 to 2007—he served during the litigation wave that swept California's Catholic dioceses and resulted in hundreds of cases and financial settlements of over one billion dollars. This legal process provided an unparalleled documentation of the Church's abuse crisis.

. . . .

I grew up in the Oakland diocese. There was a law passed in 2002 in California that allowed victims of sexual abuse of any ilk—Boy Scouts, public school kids—a year to bring a suit against the entity overseeing the abuser, in this case, the Church, as long as they could show that the entity knew or should have known about the perpetrator and did not take action. The impetus for that law came from the crisis that occurred in Boston in 2002. The sex abuse crisis has been going on in the Catholic Church for decades, some would say for centuries.

I'd been abused in the late 1960s and early 1970s, as had a couple of my brothers. There are four boys in my family; we're Irish Catholic. We had a very strong connection to the Church. I hadn't ever repressed what happened. I just didn't want to deal with it.

This priest, Father Clark, was a part of our family, basically a parish priest. I think Clark's hope was that one of us would become a priest. My parents didn't necessarily support that; they weren't hard-core Catholics.

I became an altar boy, and at that time I didn't think of what Clark was doing as being criminal. I look back and I realize now it's what's called grooming. These priests, these guys who are predators, will actually spend a lot of time preparing a child to be sexually abused. In this case, he would touch me affectionately, like my uncle would touch me, so it was harmless in my mind, and I was at an age where I couldn't discern. There was nobody watching him because we were in the vestry of the church. So he had unfettered access to his altar boys as a result of his place of influence and power within the church, an implied trust that went from everybody to him, because of who he was.

He would encourage the altar boys to take off our clothes as a part of getting ready for Mass. He would pat our backs or pat our butts and tease us. He was preparing us.

We were from a relatively poor, working-class family, so we kids would work around town to earn money. I progressed from being an altar boy to being offered a job by Clark, to work in his house. My older brother had the job first, so I knew it was lucrative. This priest, who is now dead, began by paying me two dollars an hour to sit next to the phones, and he'd also feed me. After a while, he began giving me ten, fifteen, twenty dollars for showing up, whether it was for an hour or four hours.

In this predatory system, these priests know how to use gifts or money to get close to their victims. It's what they use to create loyalty, and they also try to create shame in order to keep the crimes quiet. Now eleven or twelve years old, I was just beginning to form as a man. I was developing muscles and growing pubic hair. Clark became interested in my body. He would come home, sometimes drunk, and before he'd pay me he'd demand for me to take off part of my clothing. Saying no to a person who has been presented as a direct contact to God and a part of your community is not fathomable. I can remember taking off my shirt and his touching my chest. I felt creepy. It didn't feel right, but I didn't know what to do. Also, the money was so much that I wanted to put up with whatever I had to within reason.

My younger brother was going to work for him also, but I didn't connect those dots until later. There was a psychology that seemed to prevent us from talking about this stuff; we didn't compare notes. This guy was one of the most constant adults in my life. I had a familiarity with him, for better or for worse.

At some point, he tried to masturbate me. He said, "Take off your pants now." So I did, and he actually jerked down my underwear and began to touch me. At that point I just couldn't take what he was doing. I'm in the minority; most kids don't know how to stop these guys. I was an independent kid, and I said, "This can't be right; this is wrong." He stopped and said, "Son, you're right; this is wrong. If I

ever do that again, I want you to punch me in the stomach. In fact, I
want you to punch me right now."

I couldn't punch this guy; he was my priest. I'd been getting
more and more uncomfortable and conflicted about going there,
money or no money, work or no work; I mean I felt guilty for not
going because I was supposed to answer the phone in case somebody
died and call him so that he'd go administer the last rites. So I had
sort of the moral issues of having been entrusted with that job. And
then there was my relationship with him and the money. Having to
put up with this physical violation was creating this internal strife,
because I had these other things that I wanted to be doing, which I
felt I had to do. But, when he did that, I put an end to it; I said this is
wrong and I stopped.

At that moment, I quit everything. I quit being an altar boy. I quit
going to church. I went home and told my father, "I'm not going back
there." My dad said, "OK." He has always respected independence,
and as we got older he respected our independent decisions. That was
one of them that, clearly, he didn't ask why, not that I would've told
him. I have no idea if I would've told him had he pressed. I know he
would've taken action, because I had to stop him from taking action
when I was older and told him what happened.

I shut it down. I stuck it in a part of my mind I didn't access
often, and I tried to forget. I didn't appreciate then the kind of emotional cancer that it was.

I went on with my life. I just didn't go to church and didn't deal
with this guy. He called once in a while, angry that I wouldn't come
to the house. I refused to go. He called drunk at times and demanded
that he needed me there and I wouldn't go. My younger brother
might've gone once or twice and didn't like it. He described later
on what was really abuse and many kinds of abuse. Only my older
brother was an altar boy with me, so we were subjected to the most
grooming. The younger ones didn't become altar boys. They noticed
something in my behavior and took it as a cue, which is really fortunate. But one of my younger brothers did go and work, and Clark

made the same effort with him. It didn't get as far with him; he got a lot further with my oldest brother. That's really the essence of why I felt compelled to, as an adult, speak out. I didn't know then that that had happened to my older brother, but I have since discovered some of what did.

When I was twenty, I got a call from my father, saying, "Your brother has been in an accident. You've got to come to the hospital." My older brother had cut his hand off intentionally. He was in intensive care.

The reason I told my father about the abuse I suffered was because the priest came to my brother's hospital room. Clark walked in, and even though my brother was catatonic, he became dangerously agitated. His heart rate went through the roof, and he began to hyperventilate.

That night my younger brother told me about my injured brother's reaction to the priest's visit. It occurred to me that what'd happened to me also had happened to him. It came to me like a bolt of lightning. So I went to see my father and told him how I'd been molested, because I wanted to help all of us understand what had happened and perhaps help my brother.

I remember having to get a hold on my father to stop him from leaving the hospital, because I was afraid he was going to kill this priest. I went to see a counselor at college and described to him what happened to me as a kid. He told me I'd been sexually molested. Until much later in my life when I went to therapy and explored the effects of this abuse, I didn't really understand how abuse affected intimacy. All I knew was I didn't like the Church or authority figures.

In 2002, reading about what happened in Boston, it erupted emotionally. The legislature in California opened a time window to sue responsible parties, and I felt, if I don't pursue this I'm not really going to feel closure.

I contacted a really compassionate woman at the diocese, Barbara Flannery, the nun who was the chancellor. She was the most powerful woman, in terms of her hierarchical position, in California's Catholic community. I sent her an e-mail saying, "I want to talk to you about sexual abuse that happened to me when I was a kid."

I knew that when I went to see these people it would be difficult. It was like walking into the oppressive power, the office of the bishop. But I really wanted to give my brother some help. After he cut his hand off, he never really could return to work. He eventually began bouncing around a series of halfway houses. He needed to be heavily medicated even to function at a marginal level. My father was chasing him all over the state trying to find and protect him. After my dad found him in a psychiatric hospital, he drove him back to northern California and arranged for his permanent disability and found an institution with some caring people running it, and my brother has been there since.

I asked the chancellor, "Have you heard of Clark? Has the Oakland diocese shuffled priests? And will you help my brother?" She said, "We believe what you say happened to you. We haven't heard of this priest abusing children. In this diocese we don't shuffle priests, and if we can arrive at a way to corroborate what you said, we'll call the insurance companies and find a way to help your family."

When my brother severed his hand, he stopped communicating with everyone. I was sitting with him one day when he was in hospital and I implored, "Talk to me." And he said, "If your hand deceives you, cut it off." It is in the Bible. "If your eye deceives you, gouge it out." And then he stuck a fork in his eye. I was able to grab the fork and pull his hand out before he did any permanent damage. I called the nurses and it was quite a scene.

Have you ever dealt with a schizophrenic disabled person—the guys on the street who walk around and talk to themselves? My brother could be that guy. It is the same sort of post-traumatic behavior seen on the streets. Only he is in a better place now; he is well supported and he takes his medication. He is also a very kind, good guy, and he is really smart. One day he said, "You know, actually, I did get touched; he touched me on the chest." That opened the door to his truth, but we haven't gotten the full story from him. We only have parts of the story, and the parts we have are terrible. I knew that he had been sexually molested, but I didn't know exactly what happened.

I described what happened to him and to me to the chancellor. She knew that there were probably more kids in the community, and she knew that it was real. She had heard it before; these guys have a similar pattern. They groom, they find weak spots, they find families where the parents don't go to church and therefore are not watching. There is usually drinking involved, and she also knew some things I didn't know. I felt like we were headed in the right direction and that the Church was going to work out something for my brother. I had done all that I could and that was kind of the way that I would find closure.

About six months later, I was reading the newspaper and saw that a priest was at trial from my town; this kid was victimized. They'd moved him numerous times. That's when I knew I'd been lied to.

So I decided to open up my case. We filed the papers, hired an investigator, and found another victim of this same priest, a kid whose family I knew. The lawyer wrote to the diocese and said, "You offered to resolve this significant damage if another victim came forward, and we'd like to meet with you about settling this out of court." The diocese ignored me. We found another victim, same pattern, different age group. We leaped the hurdles to try to settle this informally, without filing a lawsuit, and the Church ignored us. The part of me that has power became simply incensed. I said, "Fuck this; let's sue them, then we'll force out the truth." When I filed suit, I filed it as a John Doe.

As a John Doe I was getting attacked in the press, by people accusing me of wanting money. They were saying that the priest was a great and a beautiful man. I wanted to challenge these people to attack me in my name if they had the courage. I had my lawyer call the local press. I wanted to put a human face on this particular priest scandal because the process of media reporting serves to encourage other victims to find the courage to speak up.

That's how I came out. I crossed the line and said, let's take this on the chin. The next article came out, naming me, and another victim came forward. We shut down the critics.

As our trial approached we went through a significant discovery process and deposition preparation. We demanded under oath that the diocese disclose any known sex crimes, convictions, and accusations related to Clark. It surfaced that he'd already been arrested and convicted of a sex crime before he ever came to our church. Clark had been arrested and the bishop had direct knowledge of the arrest at the time of the arrest.

Most of the people I know who are sexually abused by priests are damaged, and I am damaged too. I have been blessed with a strong family, a good mind, and a resilient spirit. Even then, when I was a kid, I stopped it. There is a level of esteem that I have for myself that a lot of other survivors don't seem to have, because they feel as if they invited or caused the abuse to happen. People say to them, "Why didn't you stop it?" Those questions just add insult to an already terrible injury.

The coverup, the behavior, the reaction by the parishioners— all these things resonate in surprising ways. I have met such good people in this process, survivors as well as practicing Catholics who want to change the system from within.

I don't believe in Jesus or any god. I don't go to church, and I can't. I'm not comfortable with any situation where somebody is guiding or influencing another person's behavior.

If I were pope for one year, in connection with what I know about the sex abuse crisis, I'd go on a world tour and in every country I'd implore anyone who's been victimized to tell their stories.

LAURIE BRINK, O.P.

*Sister Laurie Brink, O.P. (b. February 22, 1961)—
a Dominican Sister of Sinsinawa—is an assistant professor
of biblical studies at Catholic Theological Union, where she
teaches courses in biblical studies. Prior to her entrance into
the Dominicans, she served as a lay volunteer in Jamaica,
where she taught in a girls' high school, worked with
victims of Hansen's disease (leprosy), and volunteered at
an orphanage run by the Sisters of Mercy.*

. . . .

I 'm the daughter of a retired navy man, so we traveled most of my life, and that certainly affected and formed how I understand myself as a person, as a minister, and very much as a Catholic.

My mother is a convert. And that is important, because there are a lot of little things about being Catholic that I was never taught, because she was never taught. For instance, we had this little statue of the bust of the Blessed Mother sitting over this little tub. I had no idea it was the holy water font, because my mother had it on the wall about eye level to her. She had no idea that water went in it. It was like a decorative piece, and I used to be fascinated by Mary and the tub. I never knew little things like that.

My earliest memory is of Morocco, because my father was stationed there. I often have a sense of being more comfortable in the Arab world than anywhere else. Being Catholic has always been a part of my identity that wasn't shared with the people around me. Because we moved frequently, we were never really in Catholic circles. In the military you're segregated according to rank. You aren't distinguished by race or religion. You're either an enlisted man or woman or an officer; my dad was an enlisted man.

When we lived in San Francisco, my brother and I played this game to see which one of us could see the CCD (catechism class) bus coming through the fog first. Through the murkiness, we could just make out the headlights. So early on, church was very mysterious and being Catholic meant getting on this spooky bus that came out of the fog and took us some other place in the fog.

After CCD, we got to go to the base movie theater; movies were about ten cents. It was kind of like Crayons for Christ; it was a very positive, a cool kind of Saturday thing to do. I always had this extremely positive sense of church, though my parents weren't terribly religious. They were good folks, and they went to church on Sunday, but the larger issues were never of interest to them.

Because my dad was in the navy we often worshipped on base; we were never really part of a parish, never did have roots in that structure. Churches on the bases are multifunctional and multidenominational. I remember on this one base when the Catholics would have Mass, the altar area rotated. One side was the Protestant backdrop and one side was the tabernacle and the Catholic backdrop. There was this kind of switch somewhere. It was functional, and it was mysterious. It was something that made you different.

When something would be happening and I couldn't do it, or, if somebody else was doing something different, my parents would say, "We're Catholic." I never quite knew what that meant.

When I was growing up in Knoxville, Catholics were only 1 percent of the population and not all people liked us. The first year we lived there, my mother was in the church choir and they came over for our Christmas party. I looked outside the window, and there was a cross burning on our lawn. This was 1976, and I was probably fourteen or fifteen. I was the first one to see it, and I was the first one to run out of the house. I remember being absolutely enraged by this, and my father pulling me away because I was so angry. I couldn't believe you could be singled out for being Catholic in such a negative way.

I was adopted through Catholic Family Services. Being Catholic was my link to my biological mother, who was Catholic. This connection to the past made me determined to stay Catholic. And I became celibate! (Not that one leads to the other!)

The cross was kind of a visual symbol for what was probably always a part of my personality. It wasn't so much social justice; things were either right or wrong. I was very dramatic about things, and if there was a cause, I'd be the first one to run up the hill with the flag. When things aren't right, someone has to say something, and I have absolutely no problem being the first one to say it and be shot. I've developed a little discretion as I've aged!

When I was nineteen, I went to Jamaica and fell madly in love with the Jamaicans. I had what could probably be called a conversion experience of sorts. Not a conversion of my faith; my faith deepened. But I was turned inside out as an American. I went down there thinking much of myself. I was the award-winning journalist who was really going to do something for the poor, and in reality everything was done to me. It was the experience of seeing dire poverty and, at the same time, the joy of people in these dire situations. I'd think, "How can you be happy? This is a hovel, you're hungry, you've nothing to wear," and they'd offer me something to eat or to drink. There was no way I could go back to being a reporter. I'd lost my edge. I'd met the face of genuine and it was absolutely stunning. That really was the pivot for me with regard to my commitment and love of the Church, and my commitment to the poor and forgotten.

One of my ministries was to visit this home for people with Hansen's disease, which is leprosy. Now I am maybe twenty-one, and I hadn't seen anybody with leprosy. I didn't even know leprosy still existed. I would visit with these folks and just kind of chat with them. These are people who had no ears, no nose, were blind, had no fingers, couldn't walk. I would sit with this woman whose name was Ms. Lillian. She had no fingers left and she would say, "I want you to write a letter to my family." They lived somewhere up in the mountains. "What do you want me to write?" And she would say, "Dear whoever-it-was, Our Father who art in Heaven, hallowed be thy name . . ." And I said, "Ms. Lillian, that is the Our Father." She said, "Yes." "You want me to write the Our Father?" She said, "Yes." "Don't they know the Our Father?" I asked. And she said, "Yes. That is what I want you to write, because it says *everything*."

Then she took my face in what was left of her hands, which were just nubs, and she was blind and she held me and she said again, "It is *everything*."

I was only supposed to be in Jamaica for six months, and I stayed for two years because I couldn't stand to leave. I loved who I was becoming while I was there.

I had a homeroom in Jamaica. At that time, the classrooms were streamed, so the least functioning students were all in one class and that was mine. I'd worked with one of them—Olive was her name—extensively the first semester, because she tended to steal people's lunches. She was hungry, and she had a terrible lisp, so I'd meet with her after class. We worked together, and she was not terribly attractive and obviously uncared for. I could say that about a lot of them, but they were my girls. We got one piece of chalk a week, and they didn't have textbooks.

When we came back from Christmas break, there was no Olive for a month. Finally, Olive came back and I told her I needed to have a note from her mother about where she'd been. So she wrote a note and passed it to another girl, and I took the note. It was addressed to me, because she wanted to tell me something and didn't know how. It said, "Please, Miss; I'm pregnant. My brother and his friends gang raped me. I have venereal disease; please can you give me money for an abortion."

Now I was all of twenty-two, so I called her out of class and asked if all of this was true, and she said yes. We went to the counselor, who was a Blauvelt Dominican: Cathy Howard. And Cathy met with her, and because she had venereal disease and hadn't been treated, we had to talk to the principal, whose decision was that she needed to leave campus and come back to school with her mother. This was a developing country; this girl wasn't coming back. Her only lifeline was this school, and she'd asked me for help. Her mother said it was her fault for not sleeping with her jeans on. I knew the mother wouldn't show up.

This was the moment at which if I'd had any hope in the goodness of institutions, I lost it. I believed we were doing good things in this school, and this was a lifeline for many of these children. I was part of it, and now I was part of another side because I had to walk her off campus—this person who'd confided in me. What Olive needed was God, and I never taught Olive about God. I never told her that God loved her no matter what. I said to myself from that moment that I'd only speak of God and to God, which is what St. Dominic did.

I watched her get on the bus and never saw her again. I realized, as the person who was going to be the next great American novelist, that I didn't need to write anything. It'd already been written. It was the Gospel. My job now was to proclaim. I was committing myself to a path because of that experience, for the sake of Olive and every single Olive I meet every single day in all the places I am. I came back from that experience, looked into Dominicans in New York, and eventually made profession with the Sinsinawa Dominicans.

For me, being Catholic isn't so much about social justice, though it's part of my story. It's about the mystery of the faith. Because I teach the Bible, it's about the sense of history that our church is much older, much bigger, much broader than the perspective we bring to it. Because I study history, I can see that it changes; it doesn't change as quickly as sometimes I think it should or I'd like it to, but it does change.

The people of God are confused. They're becoming polarized because they're trying to figure out who we are and what it means to be Catholic. Some of us, in asking the questions, are more like evangelicals and some of us are more like socialists. That diversity in the Church isn't new. We aren't always sure of the parameters anymore. When people don't know their boundaries, they can get very anxious about setting them and saying who is in and who is out.

Rather than saying that one is a Baptist or a Catholic, we're now saying that one is a good Catholic or a bad Catholic. The hierarchy is in crisis, and it has to realize that it simply doesn't have the people power to make sure that our central sacrament continues and is available. It knows that things have to change or the Eucharist will be diminished, and when that happens, how will we be Catholics?

Because I teach at the Catholic seminary, I am bound to not advocate women's ordination and not even talk about it. We are not allowed to talk about some things. This one is a formal no-no. But I trust the spirit to open the hearts and mind of the hierarchy. She can be very persuasive.

I didn't experience the enthusiasm of Vatican II, and I had no sense of what the Church was like before, so I'm not disappointed that Vatican II hasn't done everything its proponents thought it'd do. I'm just trying to figure out what it means to be Catholic. When I get a handle on that then maybe I'll have some righteous anger on what was promised and what wasn't delivered. That is part of the discrepancy with the younger folk in the Church. We were so poorly catechized that our issues are, first, ones of identity and spirituality, and second, of theology.

I was born in 1961, and I'm at the very beginning of Generation X. There is a distinction between those generations that I'm coming to see more and more.

For my generation, everything has always been in flux. There is no institution that has gone unscathed for us; we were the ones who were children during Watergate. Everything after that simply confirmed that you can't trust any institution, so we don't. I'm never disappointed that the Church hierarchy does something screwy. I wouldn't know what to do with an institution that lived up to some higher standards. A lot of Generation X folks have problems with trusting.

If I were pope, first I'd work on the outfits. (Joking.)

I'd initiate a revival. I want us to remember what it was that lit our hearts on fire to begin with; why we bother calling ourselves the Church. I'd want a year of prayer and fasting for us and for the world, for the sins we committed, asking for forgiveness from those we've wronged and making reparation as a Church. I'd want a recognition of who we are before God—that we're instruments, creatures of God. We're not God. God in God's magnitude decided to make us in God's image and we darn well better start living up to that image.

If I didn't believe so strongly in the Jesus story, I'd be Jewish in a heartbeat. The Jesus story is originally the Jewish story and the narrative of Israel and its struggle with coming to understand who it was before God. It's a magnificent story, and Jesus understood that story and articulated it in a new way for a new time.

INGRID MATTSON

Ingrid Mattson, Ph.D. (b. August 23, 1963), is the president of the Islamic Society of North America (ISNA), boasting thirty thousand members, making it the largest organization of Muslims in the region. A Catholic who converted to Islam, she is the first woman to lead ISNA.

. . . .

There were seven kids in my family. We lived a block away from the major center of Catholicism in my city, which held the church, the Catholic girls school, and the Catholic boys school. I don't think I knew there was anything other than a Catholic until I was twelve years old. All my friends were Catholic. I didn't know until I was older that my grandmother on my mother's side had been raised Lutheran and converted. My father's father had also been Lutheran but converted to marry my grandmother. It was never talked about.

Christmas and Easter were filled with tons of family, though not particularly religious. My family wasn't very pious. There was probably one cross in our house. Prayer was spotty, but we went to church every Sunday. My parents' energy was focused on social justice and activism. My father was a criminal defense lawyer.

We lived in a suburb at the end of the 1950s and early 1960s in Kitchener, Ontario. One day, my sister came home and said, I want a bike like so and so, and my mother decided *that was it*. They moved us right downtown to be in a more diverse, working-class neighborhood. It was a deliberate effort on my parents' part for us to feel a sense of gratitude for what we had.

When we were growing up, our house was filled with juvenile delinquents. There was always someone who was in trouble living with us—one of my dad's juvenile clients, someone out of work, or some ex-con hanging around. Christmas dinner at our house was the combination of Jesus and the tax collector.

Two years ago, my oldest brother, who became a criminal defense lawyer like my dad, had this client who was an international student from China, accused of murder. His roommate got high and tried to attack him, and he killed him in self-defense. He was in jail for months and depressed. So my mother, age seventy-two, went to court, put up his bond, and let him live in her house—with her—until the trial. The rest of us were freaking out, asking Mom what she was doing. She said, "Oh, no. I'm fine. I know what I am doing." She had this guy in her house for four or five months. She would take him to the police station at the end of the block every day. He couldn't leave the house without her. So she'd drag him out and go to the store.

And now he's part of the family. He was found innocent.

Community service was a real part of our life. I was in Grade 5 or 6 when I started volunteering at a home for severely disabled children.

My parents never said no when we asked to visit friends, even those who lived in tough neighborhoods. One of my best friend's mother was an alcoholic and her father was unemployed. My parents trusted that we'd be okay.

For me, church was closely associated with spirituality. I was probably the most religious person in my family. I remember saying, "I think we should pray, say grace, or something like that." I've always been the kind of person who follows the rules. But I wanted more. During Lent and Advent, I used to go to church every day.

Rather than going home for lunch, I'd go to Mass. I liked going by myself to the convent. It was very quiet and clean, whereas growing up in a big family is always noisy and chaotic.

While I was in elementary school, the Church was transitioning from the old orders to the modern, guitar-strumming nuns. That was confusing for all of us. It was nice to have nuns who actually talked to you rather than yelled at you. But it did definitely take some of the mystery out of it, and it made them less special in a way, when they took off the habit and looked just like everyone else. In a good way, the barriers came down. But I think in some other ways it also made people less respectful of what they had to offer that was unique.

Once, in high school, I was trying to get my religion teacher to explain something she just could not answer. She considered me a troublemaker for asking and sent me to the guidance counselor, who sent me to the priest. He was very reassuring but didn't give answers himself. He just said, you're all right the way you are. I think I felt that, at least dogmatically, the Catholic Church wasn't capable of providing the kinds of answers that I needed. I didn't feel I was getting a coherent framework for what they were saying. I was sad to leave, but I felt like I would be hypocritical to stay.

I stopped going to church because I realized I didn't believe in what was going on there.

By sixteen, I had left religion behind. But I kept volunteering at the Global Community Center, which worked on third-world issues.

During university, I went to Paris and I met these West African students at an antiracism concert.

That was 1986. It was the first time I encountered Arab Muslims. It was a whole new world for me, and I wanted to know more.

When I returned home, I discovered that the only place Arabic was taught was at a weekend school at a mosque. Then I met Muslims in Canada. I started asking them questions, getting engaged with them, and I started to be more interested in reading about Islam. I started to read the Koran and that's when it hit me, and it was very shocking to me. I was not interested in religion and what I thought of the baggage that went with it. So I pushed it away. I kept learning, but I really didn't want to get involved. But then I had to be honest with myself. Eventually, I realized that I had come to believe this and embrace it.

I don't know if it was a calling. I was simply being honest about what had become my inner beliefs and feelings. Islam, the Koran, the practices that I was learning, prayer—all were being transmitted by this community. I realized that these spiritual practices were being sustained by a community that I should be part of.

When I was young, I was uncomfortable with the overly realistic representational art in Catholic churches, because I felt that it was taking me away from where I felt my spiritual connection. The Koran, and the words and the images, very much connected with that naïve spirituality that I had as a child or maybe that more innate spirituality that I felt had been boxed in by the art.

I like Islam's sense of connection through generations. Tradition is important, but it is tradition in the sense of trying to reproduce the actions of the prophet Mohammed, particularly in acts of worship.

Sitting at the back of a mosque one day, I noticed my son standing beside his Koran teacher, giving sidelong glances, and trying to adjust his movement to be just like his teacher. His teacher had learned that also—studying, trying to do it just the way that he thought the prophet Mohammed had done it. I like the idea of that kind of connection, that linking over generations, and that continuity.

People make this caricature of Islam, that in Islam God is distant and transcendent whereas in Christianity, because Jesus is incarnate, it's more human, so people can connect. But that's not how we look at it. The way we look at it, like Dr. Umar Faruq Abd-Allah says, the creation is like a smooth, beautiful lake on a cloudless night where in the lake you see the reflection of the sky. You can't capture the sky but you can get such a beautiful reflection. You see the reflection and you're almost fooled by it. That's the idea of these attributes of God that are dispersed through creation and that we have to try to amplify in ourselves. The more and more we do that, the more we come to understand God. This is where I see the connection with the inspiring nuns I grew up with. I felt that their way of getting close to God was through demonstrating God's love, mercy, and compassion in the world. The nuns were all about activity and reflecting those attributes. You're experiencing a small part of love and mercy that is huge and endless. That's what gives you hope when you feel pessimistic and there is so much suffering in the world.

One of the reasons that as a Muslim I feel a sense of closeness to many Catholics is that we share the same sense that if you want to be close to God, you must demonstrate love.

Women complain about their mosques, about their lack of representation and space, and I say, "No taxation without representation. Why are you donating to them? Why are you cooking for their potlucks? Use that power of your voluntary work, of your money, to tell them, 'This is our community too; either recognize us as part of it or we have to find a community that will.'"

As a Muslim, certainly after September 11 I felt ashamed. Not that we have any responsibility for it, but just for it to be done in the name of Islam was so terrible and so shameful. That was devastating for my kids too. They were very unself-conscious Muslims. But suddenly they felt the self-consciousness.

Every child grows up with challenges, but I see the difference in someone who feels discrimination. There was a significant amount of time where my son would come home from school and the teacher would be mad and he'd say, "They're racist." And we'd say, "No, you weren't behaving well in the class." We didn't want him to get used to using that or seeing that in everything.

But it's the reality of America: Racism is strong.

The Koran describes paradise in all sorts of ways—as a beautiful, luxurious place with gardens and rivers, a place of comfort and ease, where people will have purified companions. But there are all sorts of other descriptions. People are attached to whatever resonates most with them. For me, there's a statement in the Koran that there will be no idle talk and I love that idea.

There is a description of the people who die and, for some people, when their soul comes out, if they're very attached to the bad things of this life, it's a very painful process. But for those who have been working to seek the pleasure of God, it's just this very easy, smooth transition. The more you experience God in your life here, the more you're already there. It's not really this big cut-off point. It's something that you are getting closer to all the time.

The biggest challenge of our time is militarism, and if I were pope I'd like to see what would happen after a year of a complete withdrawal from anything that has to do with militarism. We should put the same money, time, creativity, and thought that we're putting into waging war toward resolving conflicts peacefully and addressing the grievances of the people. I think this is the major moral issue of our time.

J. BRYAN HEHIR

Bryan Hehir (b. August 22, 1940) is a Catholic priest and leading thinker on ethics and foreign policy. Hehir is the Parker Gilbert Montgomery Professor of the Practice of Religion and Public Life at Harvard University where he has served as dean of the Divinity School. He is also the secretary for social services and the president of Catholic Charities in the Archdiocese of Boston. Hehir's teaching, research, and policy work in the Church over the last thirty years has focused on Catholic social teaching, the role of religion in American society and in world politics, and issues of social and foreign policy.

. . . .

I grew up in a small town north of Boston. My mother and father were both deeply religious people. At the end of every day, my father would walk past our house and make a visit to the church.

My grandmother was from Ireland and a pillar of the church. My job was to take the roses from her garden to the church every holy day. I went on the altar when I was eight and was on it until I was seventeen. But I never really thought about being a priest. I just thought about being Catholic. I had no Catholic education. I went to public schools.

After my sophomore year at King's College in Pennsylvania I went into the seminary in Boston to find out whether I should be a priest. I remained interested in politics, and my professors introduced me to the famous Jesuit John Courtney Murray, who was at that time the leading theologian in the United States. Murray wrote the "Declaration on Religious Liberty of Vatican II," which was the Catholic Church's definitive declaration that it supported the right to religious liberty. It was his theological view of the world that made me feel it was possible to combine the priesthood with an inclination toward politics. I went into the seminary in 1960 and was ordained in 1966, so I was there in the midst of Vatican II. Pope John XXIII's *Pacem in Terris* was just three years before I was ordained. I remember reading it. That's the whole encyclical on peace. He talks about how you build peace interpersonally, then within a single nation, then between nations, and then in the whole globe. It's the finest of the encyclicals of the social teachings.

Acting in society is what the Catholic social teaching is about. If you take St. Paul's Epistles, the Epistles to the Romans, Epistles to the Galatians, they're almost always divided into two parts. The first part says this is who you are as a Christian; this is what has happened to you because Jesus died and rose and you have been baptized; let me tell you about your identity. The second part of the letter is always St. Paul trying to straighten out the moral problems of the local church. How local churches should deal with the state; how they should deal with each other; how they should deal with marriage; how they should deal with kids. So it's faith, our identity, and our moral life, our action. It's not only what we believe but how we should act, personally and in society. How you should act in relationship to your civic responsibilities as a human being, politics, economics, law, war and peace, international relations, and government. That's what's contained in Catholic social teaching.

How do we access it? We put it into religious education programs and the teaching of Catholic faith and Catholic schools. At least at the major Catholic universities and colleges today, it's now being taught extensively.

After the pope was shot, he went to visit Mehmet Ali Ağca in jail, and the headline on one of the magazines was "Why Forgive?" Forgiveness doesn't mean forgetting about the injustice. Forgiveness means defining the injustice, so it is clear what was done was wrong. You look at what happened in an individual relationship, in a political setting, and when somebody violated somebody else's basic human rights.

We learn to forgive by being forgiven. We can't earn forgiveness. It's not like me paying a fine to the police department and then saying, You've got nothing on me. I come before God and that which weighs upon me is lifted from me, even though I can't earn it, I don't "deserve" it. But the experience of being forgiven I think transforms a person into being a potential instrument of forgiveness.

You have to distinguish for the people between their feelings and their act of forgiveness. Lots of times people will come to you and say, I can't forgive so and so and I want to. Often this involves family kinds of things, because they're so concrete. And I always say, forgiveness lies in the will. So if you want to forgive either because you feel you ought to or because you've been forgiven, if you want to forgive and you do forgive, you can say that to yourself: then, forgiveness has occurred. You may need to grow into that act of the will. Your emotions follow the will.

In South Africa, Chile, Guatemala, and other post-conflict countries, Truth and Reconciliation Committees (TRCs) were formed to grapple with the past and prepare for the future. Often, TRCs say we as a society must bring the violations to light, declare the violations wrong, and agree that they should never happen again. But in so many of these cases, society has said no reparations and no punishment were needed.

Why forgive if there's no conception of faith? Harder, not impossible, but harder. It takes a person with a strong moral sense.

In Catholic theology, death is the journey from grace to glory. What that means is, we now see God face to face.

Until our final act of death, there's never a moment when we can't take back our assent to God. The only moment when we make an ultimate act of faith is the final act by which we grasp God and go from this life to the next. Once we encounter God, then nothing that is not of God attracts us anymore.

I've had disagreements with the people in the Church hierarchy, and I ask myself, what's the point of disagreement? How did I get here? What do I know about what the pope is trying to say or teach? Where do I get my sources of disagreement?

I had my disagreements over the contraception teaching. Paul VI's document came out two years after I was ordained. I've always lived in a parish. I love to hear confessions. I've always dealt with a lot of people struggling with this question and other questions too. But this was a huge question of disagreement in the Church. I've taught seminars on it, so I've tried to examine it myself, to teach it. When I disagree, I feel I have an obligation always to try to explain the teaching of the Church as the pope teaches it, so that I fairly represent it. I can then indicate to people where my sources of disagreement are. I have to be very careful, because I have different roles: I'm a teacher, I'm a preacher, I'm a confessor, and I'm a counselor. I don't want to represent what's going on as me against the pope. That's out of order. But I can't say I'm convinced when I'm not convinced.

The standard model for this has been, particularly for people who are theologians, if you disagree, you do not publicly state your disagreement, and you continue your research. If you're convinced that the Church is wrong, you do the research that you think would correct it, and you submit that to people who have the power to look at it. There have been cases where teaching was changed. John Courtney Murray changed the teaching on religious liberty.

Being pope is not a job to be desired! This discussion is purely a thought experiment.

I'd try to imitate different aspects of different popes of my lifetime. John XXIII had this wonderful way of opening the Church to the world and opening the world to the Church. Paul VI was a favorite of mine. I thought he was a wonderful diplomat. He really understood world affairs and world politics. John Paul II combined this overwhelmingly powerful personal faith with deep social leadership. When you watched him, you had a sense that this was an honest to God mystic. He could be in a crowd of thousands and get lost in prayer. He combined that with a terrific social mission running across a whole set of issues. That kind of mix of intellectual and spiritual is very important. This pope has proven to be a great teacher. He has a very different but very attractive style. I thought the first encyclical was a terrific piece of work. He has a wonderful way of communicating the content of faith. It doesn't have the kind of structured edge to it, but it has a more meditative tone. So, I'd like to be open to the world, I'd like to combine social and spiritual, and I'd like to be able to teach the faith in an appealing way.

KIKI KENNEDY

Kiki Kennedy, M.D. (b. June 9, 1959), serves as assistant clinical professor at Yale University, Department of Psychiatry, and has been a private practice psychiatrist in New Haven, Connecticut, since 1991. Born to Presbyterian and Jewish parents, as an adult, Kennedy converted to Catholicism—the religion of her husband and their children.

. . . .

My mother was a Presbyterian and my father's family was Jewish, so growing up I attended a Jewish youth group and went to a Presbyterian church. As an adolescent, I considered converting to Judaism but never felt that much of a pull.

When I married my husband, who is Catholic, there was absolutely no pressure for me to convert, although I did go through the Pre-Cana process with him. We decided, mutually, to raise our children in the Catholic faith. When my first child was born, I started to think about wanting to have more spirituality in my life. And then each of my parents, although in good health, unexpectedly died within eighteen months of each other and I found myself truly longing for some spiritual resource to help me cope with and find meaning in their deaths.

I understood that there wasn't going to be a lightning bolt from God that would come down from heaven and suddenly inflame me with faith. I realized that like everything else in my life, faith was something that I needed to put work into. Whether it was working to become a doctor, working at being a good enough mother, working to have a rich and satisfying life with my husband, working to be a good friend, working to be a good teacher to my students, or working to be a good activist in my different environmental and other community activities, I realized that faith was something I needed to put time, energy, effort, study, and myself into.

It made the most sense to pursue the faith that my husband had already chosen and that I'd chosen for my children. I had support from my husband, but by no means was he pushy or insistent. He never expected this to happen; he was very generous, open, and supportive of whatever I wanted to do. However, I did experience some opposition from friends of mine, who felt that I shouldn't become a

Catholic because of some of the Church's messages about different issues at that time.

I started attending Mass weekly with my children and husband. For a year, I attended weekly discussion meetings with a teacher and several other students. I studied both the assigned readings and essays that friends of mine—who aren't priests but who've been involved with the more educational teachings of the Catholic Church—suggested.

I feel very positive about my decision to become a Catholic. Even though I still haven't developed a deep well of personal faith, I do feel a growing closeness to God, an openness to his ways of working, and a sense of increased meaning and fulfillment in my life. Becoming Catholic has opened up a new way of being closer with my husband and children and members of my husband's family that hadn't been available to me before. I'm continuing to attend Mass and continuing to work on my spiritual journey. I'm still learning how to open myself up to let spirituality and faith into my life, to enrich my relationships, and to deepen my life.

ANNE BURKE

In 2006 Anne Burke (b. February 3, 1944) was appointed to the Illinois Supreme Court. Throughout her career in public service as a children's advocate and legal professional, she has provided a voice to society's most fragile citizens.

For more than two years, serving as interim chair, Burke directed the National Review Board of the United States Conference of Catholic Bishops, investigating the causes and effects of the clergy abuse scandal and helping to establish guidelines and policies for effectively responding to this issue.

. . . .

I was born into a Catholic family, the youngest of four. My dad was a bartender, and I think we were a very regular Catholic family. We all went to Catholic school and were shaped by the culture and discipline of Catholic life. After graduating from Maria High School, I went to George Williams College. During the first year of college I took a Protestant Bible history class. I'd never really read the Bible, except for the Gospels in church on Sunday. I began to have lots of questions about what I was learning. So I knocked on the door of my parish priest, Father Sweeney, and asked if he could sit down and talk to me about this class. I was consumed with why I had no previous knowledge of the Bible. He said, "I don't have time for you." I was so angry I actually stopped going to church for a while. It was the first time I'd ever asked anything from the Church, and I was really hurt that I'd been let down by my parish priest.

I didn't really go back until I started dating Ed, the man who would become my husband. He and I have always been committed Catholics; we're regular churchgoers—always there on Sundays and holy days. Ed goes every day of the week, no matter where we are— even in China. Because my husband was in the seminary for a period of time, we've always had a lot of friends who are priests.

When the *Boston Globe*, in January of 2002, began to disclose the details of the sexual abuse of minors in the Archdiocese of Boston by members of the Catholic clergy, the ensuing sex abuse crisis had a ripple effect across the nation. Day after day the reaction of Cardinal Bernard Law and the officials of the Archdiocese of Boston began to enrage the very ordinary Catholics of Boston and the United States. These issues weren't going away and it was reaching the crisis point.

Pope John Paul II summoned the cardinals of the United States to Rome and the president of the U.S. Conference of Catholic Bishops

(USCCB), Archbishop Wilton Gregory. They had a lot of explaining to do. They returned knowing that during the national bishops' meeting in Dallas, Texas, the following June this crisis had to be addressed.

A group from the USCCB and their media and public relations firm came up with the idea for a charter that the conference might adopt at its June meeting that could be seen to safeguard children and young people throughout the United States. It was aimed at out-lining, in clear language, a uniform policy with regard to how the bishops across the country, diocese by diocese, would handle abuse issues by the clergy.

The charter was unprecedented.

At a moment in which credibility was dissolving for the hierar-chy around the country, the laity seemed like a pretty good first line of defense. So they appointed a lay review board that would have the muscle to enforce the charter and evaluate how dioceses around the country were implementing it.

Frank Keating, then the governor of Oklahoma, was the chair; I was the vice chair; and Bob Bennett was the third member. It was June 2002, and we had our work cut out for us.

We expanded the board and set up an office for child protection at the USCCB office in Washington. We set out to find the best indi-vidual for the position. As soon as we began this part of the process I think we began to run into some resistance from the bishops. Once we'd identified Kathleen McChesney, the number-three official in the FBI, as our top choice for the position of director of the Office for Child and Youth Protection, I think the bishops realized how seriously we were taking our responsibilities. We started having problems with individual cardinals and bishops who thought we were too aggres-sive. We made no apology and went on with our work.

Resistance in some places was almost instantaneous. The bishops weren't used to being asked questions about their effectiveness. The whole issue of the sexual abuse crisis made many of them squirm. I think it is fair to say that some of them were part of the problem when it came to coverups and hiding perpetrators. Nobody had ever questioned them before. They were shocked, indignant. But it was all part of the public record by then, and so they were pretty much against the wall, because we were independent, competent, and determined. We were going to continue our work despite their resistance.

In addition to establishing the Office for Child and Youth Protection and all the responsibilities attached to that office, the review board was also charged by the charter to commission two studies. One was a statistical analysis relating to the gathering of accurate and pertinent information concerning the crisis. We needed to collect concrete facts diocese by diocese. We needed to know how many victims there had been and we needed to know the number of offenders, and we needed to know how long these instances of abuse had been going on.

The second study was an epidemiological study examining the causes and the context that contributed to the crisis itself.

The review board felt that it was necessary for us to issue our own report based on what we uncovered. Someone asked me why the FBI was necessary. We told him, "They know how to get their questions answered." We knew that the FBI would get to the truth in every diocese.

The bishops have a historical obsession with control, and having twelve strong professional laypeople looking under the tent, you might say, gave some of them sleepless nights. I only wish the terrible scandal kept them awake.

We were slow to expose all the details of what we were doing. In big brush strokes we were following the charter. But in the small detail, we would travel around the country and talk to people. Chancery staffs, bishops, victims, and perpetrators. We were never interested in just being window dressing for the bishops. Cardinal Edward Egan was offended by our insistence for independence. I also think he was intimidated by the thoughts of fifty former FBI agents doing our questioning. His animosity reached an absurd level when he publicly uninvited us from attending the Cardinal's Annual Gala in New York.

Honestly, at times we needed things like that for laughs and to keep our sanity.

When we were wrapping up our work we decided that we wanted all the Catholics in the pews, every layperson in the Church, to receive something from us on what we were doing, on what we discovered. When the bishops heard of this, they refused to allow it. So we held a press conference instead to get the word out on our findings and get it to the public. I think they could only abide looking in the mirror and seeing their own princely selves. But as we always said—it's not their church; it's not our church; it's Christ's church.

Frank Keating was our first review board chairman. It's no secret that he left the board very publicly just before the end of the first year. Frank just could not handle the bishops' pettiness and machinations. So he made a very public comment in the media that the bishops were like the "Mafia."

Whatever we may have felt behind the scenes, the board just couldn't stand behind such a public gaffe; it would have paralyzed us in our future relations with the bishops. The board was very honest with Frank. It was time for him to go.

The board was very clear with me that it wanted me to take Frank's place as chair. But this is the most amazing part of the story. All we ever could get out of the bishops was that I would be the "interim chair."

I believe that the bishops knew they'd have a fight on their hands if I was passed over, but there was no way they were going to appoint a woman to the position of chair. So they did what they do best—nothing.

Among the more bizarre episodes of our work was something that took place when we did the interviews for the Archdiocese of Chicago. I was a part of the team that spoke to my own archbishop, Cardinal Francis George. Among the issues was one concerning bishops who transferred priests who'd been accused of abuse. We brought it up with the cardinal. All those transfers aided in covering up many perpetrators' crimes. During our three-hour interview, Cardinal

George stated strongly to us that he had taken care of all the abuse cases. He reiterated that there was nothing to worry about in Chicago.

Then the very next day I get a phone call from a reporter asking me for comments on the headline that a priest who was accused of abuse in the state of Delaware had been transferred to Chicago and was actually living in the cardinal's residence. This was a total shock to me.

I called Cardinal George and said, "We asked you about transfers, oblivious to the fact that you have this man living with you in your home. Why didn't you say something to the board? Why would you have somebody live with you who's been accused of abuse?" The cardinal went on to say that he didn't think it was necessary to tell me that type of thing. According to him, the man was doing good work for the archdiocese. I was furious at his casual attitude.

The cardinal told me he received a letter from the priest's attorney saying that the priest in question hadn't been convicted of abuse. I said, "You mean there is a difference between the conviction and the plea agreement?" "Yes," he said. "He wasn't convicted." And I said, "Really? Do you know that when he entered the plea agreement he admitted he was guilty of the conduct of which he was accused?" "Yes, he did enter into an agreement," the cardinal said, "before he was a priest."

The cardinal wasn't honest with me. Perhaps he was not honest with himself. But just when you think these bishops are getting it, they turn around and do something that in any other enterprise would result in their own dismissal.

I found the cardinal's lack of honesty really difficult to deal with. How do I go on to trust what he says to me? This continues to the present day. He and his brother bishops have been in denial all along.

It's the culture of the administration of the Catholic Church in the United States that permitted a climate of coverup to go on for the past fifty years; it's the same culture and it's still out there today. Things have hit rock bottom in the Catholic Church, and it's going to get worse. There's a pernicious cynicism that permits it to be repeated over and over. And to make matters worse—it's OK to lie for the good of the Church.

What is the answer to all of this? What can ordinary believers do? I think it is up to the laity of America to stop and say, "Enough is enough." We want the truth, not lies. We want justice, not abuse. We want men of faith, not third-rate CEOs, to lead us to Jesus. What has occurred here with the scandal shouldn't be seen as a crisis of faith but rather a crisis of leadership.

The board went to Washington, D.C., in anticipation of the official publication of the report that was conducted by the John Jay College of Criminal Law. This included the findings of the great investigation and the hard facts of the abuse scandal—the real numbers of priest abusers and the real number of reported accusations for the last half century. It was national in its scope. No one had ever gathered the true numbers. Also to be included was the dollar amount that the scandal had cost the Church.

I was just about ready to speak before this room full of men, sixty-four cardinals and bishops, and one or two religious women, when one of the cardinals fires three questions in a row at me in a most belligerent manner.

I was just furious. So I stared at him, and then I turned and stared at Bishop Gregory, who was chairing the session. I took a breath and said, "This is how we're going to proceed. I am going to give my report. I will have a conclusion. And, at that time, if there are any questions, we would be happy to answer them." And I proceeded. It was stunning. I refused to be intimidated by His Eminence.

I easily could have been intimidated by his attitude, particularly because of his office. But we had seen too much. We had heard too much. Whatever his self-image was, he was delusional if he thought we were going to buckle under their pontifical braggadocio just as we were about to announce our findings to the press.

As a believer and a follower of Jesus, the experience of serving on the review board had a profound influence on my faith. I think many people find the whole topic of the clerical abuse scandal so reprehensible that they can't even talk about it. I was not particularly thrilled at the thought of delving into the deepest forensic understanding of what went on. But throughout my two and a half years on the board the shock of the abuse and the scandal of the crimes had just the opposite reaction in me. I think that ultimately my faith was strengthened. I came to a deeper sense of understanding of what the Lord was calling me to do. I came to rely on his presence very much in the Eucharist and in his people, those who make up his church. I came to see our involvement as a path for the Church to recover. Most of all I came to see the Church as something far wider than myself and certainly far wider than the hierarchy. My days of being a passive Catholic came to an end. And everywhere I go I encourage other Catholics to be active in the life of the Church.

The crisis came about because no one was watching what was going on. Bishops got away with concealing crime. Bishops moved abusing priests around in an attempt to make the scandal go away. They relied on the goodwill of those who were abused and their families. Nothing was ever done about the abuse until the lawsuits began to drain away huge sums of the Church's resources. Dioceses began to go bankrupt. That caught the attention of the bishops. The laity should be watchful, vigilant, and aggressive in their insistence on accountability from the bishops of their local church; and they have the right to demand real leadership from the bishops of the United States.

One of the most critical impacts of our investigation came when we traveled to the Holy See and interviewed several of the curial cardinals. Almost all were courteous; they were interested in our mission and helpful by their conversations. However, one was actually nasty and had a fit merely by our presence. He refused to acknowledge that there was any problem other than that Americans could not be trusted. What a learning experience that was.

We arrived at Cardinal Joseph Ratzinger's office to find that he had assembled his full team to hear us. I'd been warned in advance about his humble ways and charming ability to engage people. It was all true.

The cardinal was wearing a simple black cassock, one that any parish priest might wear. He had just a simple cross and his red zucchetto on his thick white hair. He had the most dazzling blue eyes I've ever seen. He came in a listening mode. Bob Bennett spoke of our effort to identify the real damage. The cardinal was surprised to hear about some of the cases we spoke of. He seemed to not have the true picture of the impact, especially those cases where financial settlements were crippling certain dioceses. I thought, "Oh my God, they have been pulling the wool over his eyes, too."

Cardinal Ratzinger's response to us was quiet and sincere. His own virtue was apparent, and he assured us that from this meeting good things could come. We knew that at least at the very top of the chain of command we had done what we could to whisper the truth into the ears that really counted.

Following his election as pope, we felt an enormous sense of excitement. Having experienced his pastoral touch up close, having witnessed his sincerity and warmth, as well as his deep concern for the life of the Church, we were grateful for his election. I'd like to think he might recall our visit and his promise to do something to ease the pain of the scandal.

It has been said that faith is the ability of our hearts to carry us further than our eyes can see. I believe that. Faith is an active virtue. Sometimes we use the wrong senses to deepen it. I am always conscious of those times when we try to make faith an academic question, as if having the right answer all the time increases faith. The right answer might make us smarter, but it doesn't always deepen faith. But I have come to know that it is the heart that more than anything else profoundly intensifies the awareness of the Lord in our life. It is the heart that pushes us out of our chair into the pain and heartache of another. That is faith.

Faith is also a spiritual experience. That is what I love so much about being Catholic; it's both active and passive; it is both outgoing and incoming. The Church has been shaped by poets, peasants, saints, the doers of justice, and the most headstrong martyrs. We have a legacy from the very time of the apostles that shows us the path to faith, which moves us along the road to holiness, which pursues us when we wander away. I love letting that dimension of our faith be a part of my life. People are hungry for the faith stories of others. People want to know the Lord. They want to know how you have found him, where you have found him, and why you look for him. This is what is so exciting about being a Catholic.

As I say that, of course, I fear for the spiritual life of my own children. I worry that they're not searching for the Lord. In many ways, can you blame them? Often, there is not much to look at in our Catholic character. I try to identify ways to faith, but my own children are often not in the mood. But I do not despair. I know that they are generous, good people. They give deeply to others. They will follow the Lord in their unique way. They are Irish and Catholic. We have a history of survival, even under great oppression.

There is an old Irish saying, "You have to do your own growing no matter how tall your grandfather was." That is good advice for families, for politics, for the Church, and for everyone who would come to know the Lord.

JOHN SWEENEY

John Sweeney (b. May 5, 1934) was elected president of the AFL-CIO at the federation's biennial convention in October 1995 and has been reelected three times since. He is the author of America Needs a Raise: Fighting for Economic Security and Social Justice.

. . . .

I'm the son of Irish immigrants. My father was a bus driver in New York City. My mother was a domestic worker. I grew up in a happy home, with two sisters and a brother. From my earliest days, I knew that I was a Catholic. My parents lived modestly but their faith was important to them. I recognized that as strong as our faith was, and the influence it had on our lives, that my father's union, the Transport Worker's Union, was also important. So there was the love of family, the strength of faith, and the support of a union member, who recognized that each contract he got might have meant an increase in wages, or it might have meant getting the forty-hour workweek or health care or another day's vacation. As kids, we understood that. I went to union meetings with him when I was in high school. He was working six days a week. I would ask him if I could go to union events in his place, and I would go around the Bronx on a sound truck with the transport workers. It was the first time I ever spoke over the microphone. I went to Catholic grammar school, high school, and then on to college. I had a great awareness of social justice and faith.

I recognized that the Church had a strong position in supporting the issues of working families and how the Church had championed the rights of workers to form unions, to have a decent standard of living, and to also help those who were the neediest. It didn't matter whether they were people in New York City, farmworkers, or people in missions of the developing world. It was with that background that I developed a strong awareness and influence through Catholic education as to what the situation was out there, regardless of what kind of a career I would pursue. The Irish Christian Brothers really raised the level of focus on treating human beings with decency and sharing with others—and because the labor movement shares these goals, I realized I could put my faith into action by working in the union movement. I understood what it meant and what it could achieve through workers organizing.

As a union member from my earliest days, working my way through college, I've been a very strong supporter of many Catholic activities. I'm a practicing Catholic. I go to Mass, sometimes during the week, but certainly every Sunday. My wife is an even stronger Catholic. She goes to Mass every day. I'm sure that my marriage has even strengthened my faith, and if I start to waver, she reins me in.

We work very closely with the U.S. Conference of Catholic Bishops on domestic policy, workers' issues, wellness, many other public policy issues, and legislation. Many bishops are very supportive. But if you look at the situation of the Church as an employer and how it treats its employees in different industries—whether it's health care or education—there's a lot that some Catholic organizations could learn about the teachings of the Church when it comes to workers, their right to organize, and their right to a decent standard of living. The teachings of the Church as they apply to human beings, their rights, and their needs should be a higher priority, but the hierarchy seems more conservative in recent years, and the seminaries no longer focus on social justice.

It's a shame because Catholics have a proud history of building our country and making it more just for working people. Irish Catholic laborers provided the backbreaking work needed for the enormous expansion of rapidly industrializing America. They ran factories, built railroads in the West, and worked in the coal mines. Irish women found work as cooks and maids in houses belonging to wealthy families on Beacon Hill in Boston, along Fifth Avenue in New York, and in most other big cities. In an era of unrestrained capitalism, Irish Catholics organized the first trade unions and held strikes when necessary for higher wages, shorter hours, and safer working conditions. From these hardworking early days, Irish Catholics quickly rose to become leaders in their communities and the nation.

Al Smith, the grandson of Irish immigrants, ascended from the tenements of the Lower East Side to seek the American presidency in

1928. As governor of New York in the 1920s, Smith originated ground-breaking social reform programs that later became the model for Franklin Roosevelt's New Deal. President John F. Kennedy, actress Maureen O'Hara, James Alton McDivitt—the first Roman Catholic astronaut to go into space—and our own Monsignor George Higgins are just a handful of Irish Catholic leaders who have contributed their talents to our country.

One of the many benefits of our multicultural nation is the joining together of Catholics from so many different backgrounds. A few weeks ago, I was with the Latino farmworkers down in Immokalee, Florida, with Ethel Kennedy. It's a very Catholic community, very strong in their faith. Before the priest said Mass, he said hello to everyone, knew them all by name. I was proud to have the experience of seeing people like that and there are thousands of people like that. I find such personal connections strengthen my own satisfaction in terms of the work that I'm doing. I was really happy to be there and proud of these people who, as Catholics, are doing such great work.

I remember going to Mass with Monsignor George Higgins, César Chávez, and Jesse Jackson, who said to me, "You can't help but be proud when participating in a religious event that's celebrating an outstanding human being and recognizing that all of these people are committed in terms of helping the farmers have a better life."

We're very strong on empowering women. As a labor movement, one of the fastest-growing segments of our membership is the increase in women workers. They're strong activists and strong leaders. I've attempted to strengthen our women representation at every level in terms of leaderships and programs. I'm always happy when the Church makes some advance in focusing on women's issues.

My faith is always a source of strength for me. There's not a day that goes by that I don't pray that the work that I do is productive and helps to reach the goals that I've set for myself. I've been very fortunate to have achieved the position that I have in the labor movement. I've worked very hard. I've had tremendous support from a lot of people. From the earliest days of my local union, there were fifty thousand members and now it's about seventy-five thousand. The principal officers were about thirty years older than me, but I work hard and they appreciated it and supported me. My career has been very rewarding and I've been blessed in both my public and my family life.

If I were pope, I'd probably make sure that Cardinal McCarrick didn't retire. That'd be perfect.

Robert Drinan

*The Reverend Robert Drinan (November 15, 1920–
January 28, 2007) was a Roman Catholic priest who
played a unique and historic role in American public life
as a lawyer, law school teacher, opponent of war, advocate
of human rights, and as a congressman who recommended
the impeachment of President Richard M. Nixon. He was
dean of Boston College Law School and a law professor
at Georgetown University Law Center for the last twenty-
six years of his life. Drinan's consistent support of
government antipoverty programs that included abortion
access drew significant opposition from Church leaders
throughout his political career.*

. . . .

I was the youngest of three people in a family that was Catholic, in an overwhelmingly Catholic community in the 1930s. I had six years with the nuns in parochial schools and then public schools. I went to Boston College, so I knew about the Jesuits.

You don't decide to become a priest. It's a grace from God. Christ, at the Last Supper, said, "You have not chosen me, I have chosen you." A lot of people reject the invitation. Remember the story in the Gospel of the rich young man. Christ said, "Go and serve the poor." And the man walked away because he was very rich. Well, I wasn't very rich, and I was lucky that everything conspired that I did become a Jesuit.

To live the life of an apostolate, to develop the mystic theology and to be a scholar and an academic and not to be just a parish priest—though that is wonderful—but to be a thinker for the Church—that's what the Jesuits have done for five hundred years. That was attractive to me.

I made a very rational and difficult decision when I joined the Jesuits. It was giving up marriage, giving up my will. When I was in college the questions were: Should I do it? Do I really believe this? Ultimately, you say yes, I believe this and it's important that I become a priest; it's sheer faith. When the apostles were approached by Christ, and he said, "Come with me," they went.

To become a Catholic and to be a priest, you commit yourself to social justice. Even before God, you look to the poor. You'll find God in the poor. Christ shows that when he goes to the poor and knows those who are in difficulty—the Good Samaritan. St. Francis of Assisi divinized poverty. This is where you find God more than anywhere else.

I had this invitation to run for Congress in 1970, and before that

I was not political at all. I'm an activist of social justice because I believe. The life of faith means that you're promoting social justice and if you believe in social justice you also believe in faith. These are inseparable. The first commandment and the second commandment go together, and the first commandment says you love God with all your heart and the second says that you love man. They are inseparable and Christ meant that, and some centers in the Church didn't quite see the connection, but Vatican II said more than ever before that we believe in the poor. That is the central tenet.

The Church is not this visible thing that we see with bishops and so on. The Church is the mystical body. It's the bride of Christ. If God has weak people running it, so be it. The Polish pope apologized for ninety-two terrible things that the Church did through the centuries. The Inquisition, the Crusades, the persecution of the Jews, all of those things, and they were done by fallible men. I assume that we can expect more mistakes to be made.

I know a few bishops who are good people. They were chosen for this position of leadership by their peers, and they recognize that especially today in America we don't like authority; we just don't blindly follow, we are an antiauthoritarian society, which is a good feature. The Church has made all types of mistakes and the Church is more perfect now in many ways than the Church in history. The pope, with whom St. Ignatius had to negotiate for establishment of the Jesuits, welcomed the Jesuits and said, famously, "The thinkers of God are here." The pope had four children, and he appointed two of his nephews to be cardinals. But St. Ignatius saw the pope and said, I want to form the Jesuits, and he had the good sense to say that the Jesuits were a whole new spiritual force.

We have expected priests and bishops to be wonderful and generally they are, but when we see somebody abusing authority, we, especially Americans, are very sensitive to that. This country was established to protest the abuse of authority and that that's in our bones is a good thing.

Don't be angry at the whole Church; talk and pray and say this is the Church of God and it is making mistakes. How can we change it? You can pray and it changes things. It might change the mind of the pope, who knows? Don't leave the Church; that's a profound mistake.

Access to abortion is another division in the Church. Everybody is pro-life, but the adamant pro-life people can get very ugly sometimes. They say we have to recriminalize abortion. That's wrong. It wouldn't work.

Women on Medicaid can't get any financial assistance. They're not as fortunate as women who have their own health insurance and can get abortions. It's just basically unfair to poor people. If we had a perfect plan, would there be fewer than forty million abortions around the world? Can we educate? (*Phone rings.*) That's the pope calling, telling me to shut up!

The only hope I have heard lately is that Pope Benedict asked people if we could revive the ancient order of deaconess. They could do that easily and these women would have wonderful roles in the Church.

God speaks to us in many ways, and I have been talking lately and writing about the Abrahamic religions and that Mohammed in AD 615 said that God has spoken to mankind, Abraham, Moses, and Jesus, and that Mohammed is the last prophet—God has spoken. Well, for a long time, we weren't very nice to the Jews and the Muslims, but they were in the same tradition. God spoke to them. God is speaking to every soul in diverse ways and do they resist? Yeah, we are geniuses at resisting grace.

It is not entirely different from a family at Christmas or Thanksgiving. There are all types of people in the family. I had a mass in Boston the day after Christmas for all of the deceased members of the Drinan family. Everybody came, and we mentioned them and that bond brings us together. You are not supposed to be really fond of some of these characters, but everybody has their virtues.

I am fascinated by the faiths of all the others. I don't quite take to Buddhism very much, but I made a retreat with Buddhists four years ago. They let us in on the Buddhist way to pray, and that was

very enlightening. They said God is everywhere and that he is trying to speak to us and we are our own worst enemy, because we do
not want to listen.

I don't say the same prayer every morning. Vocal prayer is highly
recommended, but you use the vocal prayer to have thoughts of your
own. "My soul proclaims the greatness of the Lord; my spirit rejoices
in God my Savior, for he has looked with favor on his lowly servant."
Just say that, think about it, and reflect on it. "The Almighty has
done great things for me." Pray in any way that reaches God.

I pray all the time. I live in the world of God, and you do not
need words for God. The answer doesn't necessarily come to me;
that's the mystery of God. He's not going to make it easy if you're
not clear.

We agonize. What shall we do? The best way of prayer is just to
take the Gospel or to take anything in the scriptures. If you feel dis-
tracted, you cannot really pray, so just read these things. I read these
every day at different times. Whenever you have the mood to do so,
whenever you can, or whenever you just start to think, "I want to
talk to God or about God"; it just becomes a habit that you're praying all of the time. Not with words—that is the lowest. It is a good
prayer, but as the lowest form, and you speak without words and you
remember things. So you are grasping for anything that will bring
your mind back to God. It is just nonvariable communication. And
does God always answer your prayers? We do not know. And you know,
more and more, year after year, it becomes more mysterious.

Everybody is a mystic deep down, and they want to find God
somehow. Sometimes you meet lonely people, even well educated
ones, who just reject the Church. They have not found God. It is
wonderful the ways in which people search for God.

In the Catholic tradition, we say that the Bible was written and
inspired by God. But there is a big dispute. Must you believe that
Adam and Eve were really in a garden? No; this is a metaphor. But
these evangelicals just say, strict interpretation.

I'm not merely a Catholic. I'm a believer. I believe in the God of

Abraham and a monotheistic tradition. I look everywhere for wisdom. What does it mean to be a Catholic? We absorb everything. We find God everywhere.

A prayer is a response to God's presence, and that this nice priest gives you good stuff for your book. This is why the most exalted prayer is always the liturgy, the prayer arising from the unity of the people, where God's presence mysteriously abides.

There are people who relate to the unsung, to the poor, who just believe, and maybe they believe after a struggle. Everybody has a struggle to stay in the Church and to believe these things. It just does not come easily, depending upon how God tempts you. But the Church is so rich, and faith is everywhere.

LUCAS BENITEZ

Lucas Benitez (b. November 23, 1975) is a thirty-two-year-old farmworker and the founder and codirector of the Coalition of Immokalee Workers, which stops exploitation of farmworkers and has emancipated over one thousand people from slavery in the United States over the past decade. He received the Robert F. Kennedy Human Rights Award in recognition of his courageous work fighting modern-day slavery and for his leadership of the national Taco Bell boycott, which ended victoriously in 2005 with the first increase in wages for tomato pickers since 1978.

Benitez takes inspiration from Jesus, in his work, to liberate the world.

My family is Catholic. My grandmother, my grandparents—they taught their religion to my parents, and my father worked seven days a week when I was young in Mexico. I came from a big family, five brothers and one sister. My father worked in the fields and construction, but every Sunday he worked only half a day, from seven o'clock in the morning until twelve o'clock. He'd come home, tell everybody to take a bath and then we'd all go to six P.M. Mass. Every Sunday we went to church, and afterward we'd have time with my father to go to the little plaza; my father bought us cookies and ice cream. Sunday was special because it was the only day our entire family spent time together. We always had a big dinner.

We lived in a really small one-room house. We all slept together on the floor here [*gestures*] and the kitchen was right there [*points*], separated by a door.

We had running water one or two times a week, but we'd gather water in buckets and bathe every day before going to school.

We never ate meat on Fridays during Lent. Throughout Holy Week in Mexico, we did nothing in the mornings and didn't eat at all from dinner until lunch the next day. My mother said we needed to sacrifice something because Jesus sacrificed his life for us. On Good Friday, we made a procession through the streets and prayed to the images of the saints. Then we'd go home. We weren't allowed to play music for the entire week. We had to pay for the sins of the year. On Saturday of Glory, my mother always had an altar at home with all the images of saints, and when the glory opens so Jesus would go to heaven, we'd kneel down together and pray. My parents would ask, are you repentant for all your sins? Do you promise to behave better this year? And we would say yes, and they'd bless us and we'd leave one by one after they blessed us. On Sunday we'd go to Mass together.

One of my favorite parts from the Bible is when Jesus found the temple was being used as a market and he threw everybody out. Jesus, the son of God, was a person who liked justice and wanted people to have equality. Many Catholics don't want to see the reality of Jesus. But Jesus was with the poor, and that is what led me to what I'm doing now. Jesus was liberating his people from oppression. We all have Jesus in ourselves and we have to do whatever we can to liberate this world. That is what inspires me to continue.

When you're right here in Immokalee and see the injustice, you want to change it. When we started, I was working in the fields, picking tomatoes with other farmworkers. We started talking about the job and how it's difficult and how much money we were making. And somebody said, "You're making money? When I arrived here I worked and I made nothing." He went on, "The agriculture-worker employers have people to watch us and these people have arms, guns. And at four o'clock in the morning we're forced to work. I escaped from there." You hear different stories.

In the early 1990s, I was working full time in the fields, and we started the first meetings by the CIW, the Coalition of Immokalee Workers. My brother and I talked to our co-workers, and to Greg and Laura from Florida Rural Legal Services. They were really interested in the situation and they talked to the farmworkers, took notes, and interviewed people. Then Greg and Laura took statements about what was happening in the Florida fields to the people in the Department of Justice in Washington, D.C. And the guys at Justice said, "This isn't happening here in the United States, are you crazy?" So they came back from Washington to Immokalee and we gathered evidence and took the case to Miami. The FBI sent an agent around ten o'clock in the morning. He said, "I'm here to interview the victims," so I said, "But they're working right now." He said, "I don't have time to wait. I need to leave Immokalee by three to be in Miami by five." So he left.

After a lot of work to convince government officials, one lawyer in the Justice Department became interested in the case and started to investigate. Finally, in 1997, the FBI arrested the perpetrators, and they were sentenced to fifteen years for slavery. Four hundred farmworkers were freed. Since then, we've taken other cases and freed more people.

There was one priest who was very close to the farmworkers and he helped people to escape. But he was a very naïve person; he didn't know what to do with these people. He was really happy to have rescued them from this situation, but he didn't keep in contact so we couldn't find them to help prosecute the case. Today, the Church plays a very important role. The Church gives us sanctuary.

Sometimes when we've rescued people, federal agencies place them in jail for a week or two, as witnesses. They say they're protecting the victims. But that is crazy. Instead, CIW brings them to a safe house so they can return to work and live in the community. The best therapy for farmworkers is to start to work and send money to Mexico, because that is why they came here. One of the victims said, "It's like I've come out of darkness into light." The Catholic Church provided one of the safe houses; the Church has helped us a lot.

When we organized the first general strike, Bishop John Nevin of the Diocese of Venice, Florida, was really interested. When we started the hunger strike, he became more involved. He came to Immokalee, he called the archdiocese, and through the bishop of Baltimore, for the first time, the cardinal came to meet with the people taking part in the hunger strike.

This gave us hope. We knew we were not alone. Now the Catholic Church is more involved.

During the Taco Bell boycott, we traveled to California and went on a ten-day hunger strike. Cardinal Mahoney asked us to stop, saying he committed himself and his parish to support our struggle. It was nearing Lent, and so, out of respect, we agreed. The cardinal got more involved. He sent a letter to Taco Bell's CEO, as did Bishop Soto from Orange County, as well as other people from the Church.

The priest in Immokalee right now, Father Hectore Ruben, is

amazing. He supports the CIW work. He led a three-thousand-person march we organized in Immokalee, where almost 80 percent of the people are Catholic. For us, the priest symbolizes peace.

I believe that I'll go to heaven to be with God. It's a place where you'll be at rest, where you'll have time for the things you don't have time for here on earth. You aren't here physically anymore, so you might be an angel. There are hundreds of angels taking care of us, protecting us. My grandmother from my father's side, the only one I met, and my grandfather from my mother's side will take me on their laps. Sometimes I feel their presence.

I've been in harm's way, in risky situations many times, and everything has been OK. Somebody is protecting and watching over me. It's not a place to go and rest, but you'll be peaceful.

If I were pope, I'd carry the message of hope. I'd support the most noble and just causes—I'd help poor people produce things so they could support themselves. I'd help causes like ours in the CIW, to fight against exploitation. The pope has a strong voice against walls that are being built between countries and to end unfair and unjust wars. The few leaders we had have been taken away. I'd raise my voice to end injustice in this world.

Guilt is when you do an evil thing and you don't apologize, or when you bear rancor against someone who has harmed you. All the people that I think I hate after all these years of struggle, I've learned to love them. When we went on the ten-day hunger strike against Taco Bell, I was really angry with the CEO, and after that we met Jonathan Blum [then vice president of Yum Brands, parent company of Taco Bell], and I thought, this is a person, and people are afraid. He has to defend his job. At the end you see that everybody has this feeling of doing the just thing.

I don't go to church every Sunday because of my work. To practice your religion, you don't have to be physically in the church every Sunday. I haven't felt far away from my religion, because I'm always close to my saints and also this cross and medal with the Virgin

Mary around my neck. It's always with me, wherever I go; I'm always reminded of them.

I believe I'm fulfilling on earth what I was sent for by God. The bishop told me, "You're doing the work God wants you to do, giving voice to people who don't have it. That is why we've recognized your work, and you're the image of God."

ALLOUISA MAY THAMES

Allouisa May Thames (b. October 8, 1988) is a freshman at the College of St. Catherine in Minneapolis, Minnesota. She is considering becoming a nun.

. . . .

I turned nineteen three days ago.
    I was born in Georgia and lived in Louisiana and then Missouri. I went to a Montessori school through ninth grade and a Catholic high school. Right now I'm a freshman at Saint Catherine's.

When I was little I used to get bored at church. When you're five or six, you're like, when is it over? Why are we here? But in first and second grade I started to think about my faith and ask questions. That's when I started going to the parish school religion program. As I grew older I began to appreciate and enjoy Mass.

I don't like to go to Mass here on campus, because this church is too liberal for me. People stand during convocation while I usually kneel as a sign of respect. I don't feel comfortable. In his homilies the priest avoids talking about God and Jesus, like he's stepping on eggshells trying not to offend anyone. If you're going to Mass on a Sunday in a Catholic church and you don't believe those things, why are you there? My roommate and I have decided to go to Mass at my grandma's church. The priest there preaches the Gospel through what the Church believes.

Last summer I worked in a lab doing chromosome analysis, and when the ballot initiative came up I thought it was offensive that many people assumed I voted for stem cell research. They didn't take my morals into account. As a Catholic, I believe there are certain lines that shouldn't be crossed, and when you mention the words "stem cell research" people automatically go to amniotic. But that's not the only option. I know a couple of people who have been cured by their own adult stem cells, one with Hodgkin's lymphoma. There are options that don't involve the dissection of life. Those need to be explored and researched more before we decide.

With regard to birth control, abstinence of course is the best way to prevent any unplanned children from being born. Beyond that, I'm a big advocate of natural family planning. Of course, you can't plan things exactly all the time, but having a little more control over when you have a family helps.

I agree with the Church's ban on condom use. If you're in a marriage, you have to be open to life when you share that love and engage in those marital acts. When one spouse has HIV, you are putting the other spouse's life in danger. In this case the couple should abstain from sexual intercourse, because if they really love each other they wouldn't want to impose HIV on the person they love.

When you engage in that intimate act, you must give yourself fully, your soul, your everything; you can't hold something back, you must be open to that life. If you can't do something naturally, then don't do it at all.

I have a genetic disorder called tremor syndrome. To stay healthy I have to take estrogen. For me it's not birth control, because I can't have children, so there's no chance that I would be destroying a life in preserving my own health. I've come to terms with the fact that I can't have children, and my husband and I are going to have to adopt.

Women have come a long way in the Church. We're able to serve as lecturers and eucharistic ministers. When I was an altar server I had good experiences. But I don't know how I feel about women priests. There are different ways for men and women to serve but still be equal. Being a priest or being a religious sister are very equal but just different ways of serving. I'm not one who easily goes along with change.

When I was fourteen or fifteen I suffered from anorexia. I went to a faith-based treatment center, because there's no way anyone could come out of a depression like that without God's help. When you're in recovery it's like you're starting a new life. It's so freeing, you feel rejuvenated, and I want to give back this second chance, this new life, to the one who gave it to me, to God. The first thing that came to mind is becoming a sister. I'm still discerning this vocation.

Am I really called?

DAN AYKROYD

Daniel Edward Aykroyd (b. July 1, 1952) is a Canadian comedian, actor, screenwriter, and musician. He was an original cast member of Saturday Night Live, *an originator of the Blues Brothers (with John Belushi), and has had a long career as a film actor and screenwriter. His films include* 1941, Trading Places, Ghostbusters, *and* Driving Miss Daisy, *which brought him a best supporting actor Oscar nomination. As a boy, Aykroyd was educated in a Catholic seminary and he has strong opinions about Catholicism.*

. . . .

I was in Grade 3, six years old, going to the English Catholic School and the English Catholic Church in Hull, Quebec. One Sunday, my family was taken to Mass and the monsignor there—we'll call him Monsignor K—was presiding and my father went up to the railing, kneeled down, and was baptized. I asked my mom what was going on and she said, "Well, this is the day your father's becoming a Catholic." He'd been a High Anglican.

That was a vivid day. That was the day my father fully accepted Catholicism, its teachings, and his pursuit of Christianity in a new direction. He became a preacher and preached in Texas. He was a fundamentalist. He loves the Bible. As a kid, before Catholicism, he went on missions but under pressure, I think, from my mother, a French Canadian Catholic and my grandmother, he had to convert to Catholicism.

When I was nine years old, I was staying over at my grandmother and grandfather's house, and one night I was going upstairs to bed and my grandfather was on his knees with a rosary, his head bent in prayer, and above his bed was a picture of Christ. That to me was a beautiful and genuine testimony and tableau of a man's deep connection to his faith.

About five years later, I spent a spectacular Christmas Eve up the Gatineau River, which runs north of Ottawa in the oldest mountains of the world, the Gatineau hills. We rented a farm there every summer and winter. The local priest asked if I would read the lesson for the night. And a farmer sent a sleigh with horses to pick us up and we went up the highway to the little church about three miles away. The church was completely packed with people and I got up and the lectern was right next to an air vent that was blowing hot air. All the way through the lesson, I thought I was doing a really good job, but people were laughing. Apparently the vent was blowing my coat halfway up my back in this billowing wave, as if I had tails on, and after they told me what it was that was making them all laugh. That is a vivid memory of ritual, of atmosphere, and all of those things that you would associate with a great Christmas Eve and a great midnight Mass in a country church.

Then I take you to reminiscence number four. It's 1968 and I'm seventeen, eighteen years old and it is a bitter, bitter cold February night, and me and three other guys get into my dad's 1966 Ford Custom 500 and we drive over to Quebec. I heard about this orphanage that had been shut down and was abandoned and I said, "Guys, we gotta go over there and take a look at this place. Maybe we can get something for the walls of our house." So we drive over to this orphanage on the outskirts of Hull in this brutally cold blue, blue night and we come to this massive chain-link fence like you see around construction sites. Closed off and there looming behind it is this nine-story orphanage from the turn of the century, a big stone building with completely blown-out windows; they're ready to tear it down for construction.

So we clip a hole in the fence and we go inside. The halls are lined with these eerie busts of nuns with glasses on. One looks like a crow. One looks like a stork. The whole place has been trashed, the toilets are gone, the plumbing's gone. People have picked it all over but they've left these statuaries. Then we get into this one room and there must have been four hundred crucifixes just thrown into a corner, so we load the car with every conceivable bust and statue, pack it full of crucifixes and oratory and baptismal fonts, and we take them and we load them into the car and we go to our house on Metcalf Street, and we plaster the walls with this stuff! We had crucifixes everywhere and busts and statuary.

About two weeks later the house is raided because some of us were engaged in selling . . . well, combustibles you might say, so the police—the Ottawa police—send in their narcotics squad and they come in the door, no warrants or anything. They come in because they expect to find some activity. Actually, we kind of knew they were coming so we stopped everything. They get in the house and their expressions I'll never forget. These cops were silent and awe-struck. Every type of crucifix and conceivable gore was plastered on the walls; every room had a nun. And they slowly backed out of the house and went down the steps. Must be a cult, they thought. They assumed all the stuff was stolen so they confiscated it. Took it all to the police station where it was a marvel to the cops there. How could anybody have this much reliquary or iconography in one place? And they hunted around town and of course it wasn't stolen because nobody wanted it anymore.

When I came to write *The Blues Brothers*, having been through these experiences of going to the seminary, being in churches where you had really vivid depictions of the crown of thorns and the eeri-ness of the stations of the cross, it was only natural that I'd create the character of the nun. So these are the material associations of Catholicism that remain in my memory.

When I finished grammar school, my parents decided that they wanted to put me in the Catholic school system in Ottawa because they thought the public school system in Hull was not quite right. They thought I'd get a better education there. They sat me down and said we're going for an interview, you'll talk to Father Lenny there, and he'll ask if you would consider a career in the priesthood. You'd better answer yes if you want to get into this school. So we went to the school and Father Lenny said, "Well, Dan, we're consid-ering having you come here to be one of our students. Do you think a career in the priesthood is something that would interest you?" And my answer was, "NNNOOOOYeaaaahh, sure, sure," because my par-ents really wanted me to. I went there for four years and was a com-plete ringleader, breaking out of the dorm at night and having girls over to the dorm. The seminary sent a letter to my parents saying, "We feel that Dan is not really suitable for the priesthood."

I then went on to a mixed school and got introduced to girls—Catholic girls in the classic white blouses and plaid skirts. From then on there was really no more overt religious training. I stopped going to church. I went to Carleton University, where I studied criminology, and then went into show business.

My stance today is that one doesn't need religion to lead a spiritual and moral life. I believe in the afterlife, but I believe it as a bio-scientific fact. I think the soul lives on, but I don't think it has to live on in a Catholic sense, a Buddhist sense, or a Hindu sense. We are born with consciousness. And then experience tumbles into that, and we are conscious of experience, and then you take consciousness and experience and that equals self-identity and self-determination.

I believe that consciousness plus identity and self-determination is where you're going to come to some kind of crossroads morally. You don't need a religion to be ethical and moral. When you kill, you then cross a moral line. When you steal, you cross a moral line. But to covet, to have envy, to have greed—these are just vulnerabilities that one has to deal with in one's life. So Catholicism is no longer necessary for me to lead my life and lead it in a moral and ethical way. I am extremely ethical, and I am a moral person, but I don't need Catholicism in my life today.

When I went to the Vatican, I thought that it was one of the most frightening places I've ever seen. We were in Rome for *Blues Brothers 2000*, and I just got the history of the Church. You think back to those corrupt popes, when they were sleeping with their sisters and daughters, and the power of these statues. I imagined these poor farmers and poor Italian people coming in over the hundreds of years and seeing these massive looming marble statues and then going away and giving half their fortune to the Church. I absolutely believe the Vatican works on the scale of a separate government, a separate country, and is capable of tremendous crimes.

Where my affection is still maintained is the front-line Catholic Church—the local church, that poor local priest there who gets nothing.

You see these poor priests trying to make it in communities— rural and urban—all over the world, and they're getting nothing from the head office. They can't even put a roof on their church. They barely have vehicles to drive. They have initiatives that are totally supported by the parishioners and nothing comes down from the head office. Even your Burger King franchisee does better than the franchisees in the Catholic Church.

I do appreciate church architecture, the architecture of the Vatican, of these basilicas and cathedrals. It's quite impressive, but there definitely was a deliberate imposition of style, grandeur, and scale that was at work to keep the parishioners and the attendees in their place. I'm conscious of that when I go into these magnificent churches and cathedrals and am made to feel smaller than God, when in fact we're part of God and we should feel an equality with that energy.

I go to church occasionally in the summer. I like to make it in there once just to support the local priest, let him know I'm part of the community. I have sympathy and love for these priests and sisters who are on the front line. I will give my love and I'll give my money. I put a roof on our Catholic church locally, and I'll support my local church because I respect that some people need this ministry in their lives.

I think God is in all of us. God is a universal force that has a spark in everything from the smallest mosquito to humankind. And when we commune and do good things in the world, that's God and good works in practice. I just can't restrict my notion of God to a figurehead or an iconic image.

I'd embrace gay and lesbian priests, because I don't believe homosexuality is immoral. I draw the line at bestiality because it's unfair to the dog or the cat. If the dog or the cat had consciousness, then that'd be OK with me. Sexuality has nothing to do with morality. I admire Christ. Whether he was in reality the son of God or not is irrelevant to the values he's brought to the world in little codes like "To those whom much has been given much will be required."

I flip through the Bible occasionally. I like the Old Testament for all the slashing and burning, and fornicating and all that, 'cause it's adventurous. I love the Christmas story. But I'm not overtly religious in any way, and I'm not out there crusading. I will say the values of Christ are vital to our world. It's really all we have left in terms of treating people humanely.

To get in touch with my spirituality, I get on the motorcycle and ride. I feel the earth and the wind—just the miracle of symmetry in everything, the grandness of nature, its randomness, its chaos, its joy. I think that I see spirituality in animals and plants, and also I guess I draw inspiration from the works of others. When I see good works being done in a community, I want to help out. And spirit is a very personal thing. For me, it's linked to just the life force on the planet and getting in touch with that. Plowing, trying to project loving energy, trying to suppress anger and my bad temper; I think if I put out positive energy, and plow that forward like a snowplow, then that's going to bounce back on the plow and bounce back through the windshield on me.

I don't envy people who are devout like Mel Gibson and have that devout Catholicism that drives them and gives them a source of power in life. I'm happy for them, but I don't wish I had that or feel it's missing.

At some point, we just have to make a choice for authority or against it. It's like the cops I've known who did acid and coke and smoked pot and now they're cops and they're enforcing the law. If you can ride the edge and have a little rebelliousness in your life and also be conventional like my father, that's great. He was an absurdist. He had a tremendous career in government, but we'd go shopping in a local grocery store and just to keep his anarchistic side alive he'd grab a roll of toilet paper and whip it over the aisle—just to hear someone yell, "Hey, what the fuck?" He knew no one was going to get hurt but that it would shake people up.

We were always taught to take care of those who were less fortunate. I went to camp one summer and I got a trophy for being the best camper, and it wasn't because I knew how to light a fire with a flint. It wasn't because I saved a sick turtle or I mastered wood craft.

It was because I identified a few of the younger campers who were being picked on and took them under my wing and made sure that they had my approval. I had a certain status and respect at the camp. That came directly from teachings of compassion, and I got that trophy because I helped those kids get through camp without having a miserable time.

In my own life, I've taught my children compassion. I don't care what they do and where they go in life, if they take compassion for their fellow men with them. I teach my kids that the guy on the street pushing the cans is no better than me and I'm no better than him. Something happened in his life to take him where he is today.

I feel guilty when I've wronged another human being. I don't feel any Catholic or Judeo-Christian guilt, except when I've hurt another human being. I was a thief, and I never felt guilty about it. This was in Canada, when I was in college. I was studying criminology and I was also in this gang of thieves. We were hijacking big meat company trucks and cigarette company trucks. At that time, the cigarette companies had the people right by the nuts and the short hairs. They were exploiting the people with a substance that was addictive and the government was charging taxes. To break open a parked truck of cigarettes and take those cartons and go sell them, we felt we were doing society a favor.

The big meat companies polluted and slaughtered hogs in these horrible ways and exploited their workers. So we stole hams and turkeys and gave them out for Christmas; that was a positive social move for me. We weren't robbing from people; we were robbing from big corporations. It was kind of legitimized at that time. I never felt guilty about that.

I feel guilty when I have to break a promise. I feel guilty when I hurt people in my family or my friends—if I've had to cross them for certain reasons out of self-absorption or selfishness.

I ain't never killed nobody, ain't never gonna kill nobody.

The person I am today was largely formed by the religion, but I don't need religion for my faith. I have my own faith. If I need to pray, I pray in my own way. I pray for people who are sick, and I believe in this concept of doing circles of prayer and calling people up and saying, "So and so is sick, let's pray for him at a certain time."

It's not necessarily calling God to do it, but it's more focusing your energy together and thinking about that person's condition, and hoping and focusing on bettering the condition. I pray in that way.

There is one thing that I really liked about Catholicism growing up—confession. Free psychiatric and psychological help. I think for the First Communion, there was some tiny little sin to confess. I went to confession all through the seminary and some of the sessions would go on for half an hour where we'd really get into some root causes of human behavior.

All of the teachers at the school were very well educated and they were really good men, so you'd go to confession and the screen would slide by and you'd go, "Oh God, it's my religion teacher, oh God, it's my math teacher. I'm going to have to tell him and he'll be seeing me in class and know." But then it would evolve into a discussion of why people behave a certain way and how to react with other human beings, and how to maybe temper reactions and cause betterment in your own life.

What happens when you die is the soul's energy goes into the multiverse, and it goes to a parallel dimension. The first stage, I believe, from what I've read and my personal belief, is one meets everyone whom one has known in life in a big reunion—like a party. Only those who have gone before are there, so when I go I'll be greeted by Gilda, John, my grandparents, and my parents, if I don't predecease them, which is a distinct possibility. And I'll see John Candy, for instance, coming to me and saying, "Ah, great to see you," catching up on things, and then he'll say, "I have to go now. I can't spend any more time, because when my soul went across they already assigned me to another entity or another function. I'm just here to welcome you across and know that at the end of this reunion everyone will vanish and you will have no consciousness of your former life. You're gonna go on and your soul energy is gonna go on to another task and be reassigned, as it were." I remember when Belushi died—in the cathedral there were three pregnant women and I thought, "His spirit has got to be going on in one or two of them." I believe in the continuity of the soul energy as a bioelectric fact, and you'll have many people debate me on that, but it's my personal belief.

Cardinal Theodore Edgar McCarrick

Theodore Edgar McCarrick (b. July 7, 1930) is the former archbishop of Washington, D.C. The U.S. Conference of Catholic Bishops (USCCB) elected McCarrick to head committees on migration, aid to the Church in central and eastern Europe, and international and domestic policy.

. . . .

I'm an only child with a large family. My father was one of thirteen
in a Catholic family from Virginia. My mother was one of eight in
a poor family from Ireland. My father died when I was three, and my
mother had to go to work in a factory in the Bronx making car parts.

My mother was brought up in the faith and at the end of her life
she became a daily communicant.

I went to Incarnation School, which had at one time between fifteen hundred and sixteen hundred students. We were split between
morning sessions and afternoon sessions. In my class, when I was six
years old, we sat three on a bench. There were seventy of us, with one
nun teaching. She had to keep us together, try to keep us quiet, and
teach us! It was a great experience and we learned a lot.

I went to Catholic school throughout. I graduated from Incarnation School in 1944 and then went to Xavier High School in New
York, but I didn't take it as seriously as I should have and was ex-
pelled. I was really disappointed with myself and with disappointing
my mother and my family. I'm grateful she was able to get me into
Fordham Prep, where I finished high school.

When we were really young, 75 percent of the boys in Catholic
school wanted to be priests. As we got older, the percentage got
smaller and smaller, and by the eighth grade maybe only five or six
of us did. I was one of them. I was an altar boy and grew up in a very
Catholic neighborhood. I didn't really know people who weren't Catholic, other than some Jewish friends.

You always have hesitations about making such a commitment;
it would be unusual for anyone not to reflect on a vocational decision
he or she has made. I was twenty when I made my decision. I was on
retreat in Switzerland at a Carthusian monastery in the mountains.
It was there that I looked at my life and felt that God might be call-

ing me to be a priest. In the seminary you go through times when you wonder if you made the right decision, but as I look back I could never imagine having done anything else.

My mother would've loved to have grandchildren, but she was good about my decision. She would ask, "You're going to be a priest around here, right? You're not going to be a missionary?" So I told her that I really wanted to be a parish priest.

If you don't have faith, then Mass becomes just a symbol. We believe it's a reenactment of the mystery of God's love, of Calvary, and of the Resurrection. What a tremendous gift when you think about it.

When I was archbishop, I would try to celebrate daily Mass in different parishes as often as possible. When talking with people, I would wonder if they knew why they were going to Mass. To a certain extent this is the reason for our preaching. Preaching has to break open the Scriptures; people have to learn what the Lord is saying, what he means, and how it fits into this life. Our preaching also has to give people a reason for the faith, share with them Jesus' words, why we believe this, and that we have to open ourselves to believe.

I offer Mass every day. If you don't have Mass in the morning, you feel like the day hasn't really started. The greatest gift we've ever received from the Lord is Jesus. He sent His son to be like us in all things except sin. The Father wants us to know He understands our lives and sent His son to be one of us. Your whole life should be moved by prayer.

I remember St. Vincent de Paul saying that it is always an insult to the poor to give them anything, but if you do, do it with love and they will forgive you. It is a great line, so when you give you give with love. Catholic social justice teaching is based so much around human dignity and was very much the key to the teaching of Pope John Paul II. To believe that God is love and that He cares for us is to recognize the dignity of the human person; I have never forgotten that. That has been a motivation in my life.

It was so good to hear the Holy Father say that you cannot be fully Catholic if you are just faithful to the liturgy and faithful to the doctrine. The doctrine, the liturgy, and praying together demand that you work on the inequalities and the disappointments of our times, that all people have a right to live and, beyond that, a right to a decent life.

I don't believe you can be authentically Catholic without being committed to the social doctrine of the Church. When I was in grammar school, we had these little boxes to help the poor. That was good, but that is half of it. The other half is to find out why there are so many poor people and how we can do something to help them. I've tried to be involved in third-world issues to make sure that today's globalization is with a conscience.

You can't be an authentic Catholic unless you're committed to the right to life. And this right is more than just being born. It involves the right to grow, to be educated, to have a family, to exercise your dignity, to work for a living, and to make a contribution to society. You can't forget about people once they are born.

If I were elected pope, I would resign right away and get a good guy in there. We've had great popes and Pope Benedict XVI is no exception. He's so anxious to serve the Lord, to follow his predecessor whom he loved so much. The secret of Pope Benedict XVI is that he's truly a very humble man. He doesn't want to be John Paul II. He wants to be Pope Benedict and to do what God is telling him to do. The humility and holiness of this Holy Father is overwhelming. He's brilliant and he's so clear. He's trying to get us all back to our roots.

I would do the same thing but not as effectively, because I'm not as smart or as holy. What the Church needs today is faith. This Holy Father is very concerned about Europe, as all of us are, because it seems to be drifting away. Europe needs that new evangelism. We have to rebuild it.

Once we get back to our roots in faith, from there we build charity. Charity is about the poor, about the social doctrine of the Church. Charity without faith isn't going to happen; without faith it's just philanthropy.

If I make it, heaven for me is that I'm going to be with the Lord and at peace. That's where we all need to be as we go through all the challenges and concerns of our life. We worry about ourselves, our families, our friends, peace in the world, people who are poor, and the future. In heaven we'll be able to say, "Lord, thank you for letting me in, for taking all these worries from me, and allowing me to be in peace. There'll be no more pain, no more tears."

There is a hell. I hope there aren't too many people going there. I hope that the God who loves us will find a moment for each one of us to say "I did wrong" and "I'm sorry." There are evil spirits in the world, but we have hope that there'll always be—for everybody, even the worst of us—a moment when the Lord will say, "Tell me, do you really not love me?" And the answer will be, "I love you, and I am sorry."

THOMAS S. MONAGHAN

Thomas S. Monaghan (b. March 25, 1937) is the founder of Domino's Pizza, the former owner of the Detroit Tigers baseball franchise, and the founder of Ave Maria University.

. . . .

My father died when I was nearly five years old. He was my favorite person, and I feel confident that he went to heaven. After that, I spent two years at the home of a German couple. They were very strict and fairly mean—spotless house, argued constantly in German. I asked them one time, "Why don't we go to church?" They said very clearly, "Because only bad people go to church." I was six years old, and I didn't buy that. My mother took me out of there so I would be raised as a Catholic, which she really got in spades, because I was basically brought up in a convent.

I was at St. Joseph's Orphanage for six years, until I was twelve. There were about eight sisters, fifty boys, and a priest living in this great big Victorian mansion.

St. Joseph's was very strict. We were taught about God all day long.

In the third grade I went to a parochial school. Sister Ladislaus was like a Marine Corps drill instructor. Everything was by the numbers. My number was twenty-five. We had to do everything in a certain way and if you did things out of order, you got in trouble. My last couple years there, I had the honor of cleaning the chapel. I attribute a lot of my faith to the fact that I spent so much time before the Blessed Sacrament.

We had prayers when we got up in the morning, went to Mass every day, had benediction every evening, and more prayers every night before we went to bed. Every room had religious pictures and statues. I hated it, but I knew down deep it was good for me.

I don't know if I ever felt distant from the Church. It was ingrained in me. I understood that I was created by God and for God and He established the Church and He set in place commandments we were supposed to follow. I had less inclination than anybody in the world to follow them, but I knew that I should. I always felt that the most important thing in my life was to be a good Catholic. When I got out of the orphanage, I kind of went wild. I went from almost a prisonlike atmosphere to unlimited access to everything. But all through those years, except for a short period of time in the Marine Corps, I never missed Mass on Sunday.

I never thought I'd marry a woman who wasn't Catholic, but I met my wife and fell in love with her. She was everything I wanted in a woman—beautiful, wholesome, sincere, and down-to-earth. I had no doubt that when she actually got instructions in the faith she would convert. She readily agreed to raise the kids Catholic and to send them to Catholic school. While she hasn't converted, she does goes to Mass with me on Sundays. Some people say she'll convert the day after I'm dead.

Now, I say at least six Rosaries a day, and I learned this from Mother Teresa. She had her sisters say Rosaries whenever they were not doing anything else, so they were never wasting time. If I'm waiting in line or in traffic, I say the Rosaries, because I feel I'm doing something God wants me to do.

I go to Mass every day. I also say the Divine Office every morning and evening. I do the Angelus three times a day. I say a prayer before every meeting, and before I give a talk I try to remember to say a prayer to the Holy Spirit to guide me, because I never read my speeches. I also pray before every meal.

I've always liked *"Thy kingdom come"* in the Our Father. I think everything should be for His Kingdom and not mine. I don't always live by it, but I try and know I should.

At St. Joseph's we learned that there is good and evil. We learned what the commandments were and what types of sins were under each commandment. I wanted to avoid the bad things.

The Catholic education of my children's generation was very different. I'm disappointed that I sent my kids to Catholic schools, because they tend to undermine the faith rather than strengthen it. They've started saying, "Well, maybe it's not a sin; it's your conscience."

My vision for Ave Maria is to be the best Catholic university we can be. It's the best way I know to accomplish my main goal in life, which is to help as many people as possible get to heaven and me along with them. We want this to be like a Catholic Princeton. Our twenty-year goal is for Ave Maria to have fifty-five hundred students—four thousand undergraduate—with SAT scores averaging 1,400, or 31 on the ACT, and comparable GPAs. Furthermore, it is our goal to have 20 percent foreign students, which will make quite a unique, diversified campus. It's important to have a high quality of excellence.

One of the largest clubs on campus is the Chastity Club, and it was started by the students. Another popular club is the Pro-life Club. More than half of our students go to daily Mass. As far as I know, from talking to students, there's not a single one who doesn't go to Mass on Sunday, assuming he or she is Catholic. About 98 percent of the kids are Catholic and we have had a few come here and convert while here. So the whole environment is reinforcing the faith. All of our faculty who are Catholics are good Catholics. Personally, I'd rather have a faculty member who's not Catholic but with our mission than have a mediocre Catholic.

We get very orthodox theologians. The students have to take theology.

My definition of a good Catholic is someone who, if he died right now, wouldn't go to hell—that is, someone in the state of grace. He'd go to purgatory and heaven. And, of course, you have to make a good confession.

Catholic guilt is one of those criticisms of liberal Catholics about the Catholic Church. I think a certain amount of guilt is good. You go to confession and you don't have guilt anymore.

Catholicism was never a barrier to my business. When I first started, I had a little conscience issue of whether I should be open on Sundays. I never believed in shopping on Sundays. It was the busiest day of the week because they didn't serve meals in the dorms on Sundays. So I asked several priests and others whom I respected, and they said, "There's nothing wrong with it."

People ask me all the time, "How can you be a successful businessman and a good Catholic too?" My answer is always that they complement each other. If being a Catholic means being good to people and treating people fairly, if you do that you're going to be more successful. What's the conflict?

I believe in the Golden Rule. I operated Domino's according to it. I felt that the most important thing I could do as a businessman was just to be honest. I never cheated the government. It's a cash business, and I turned in all the sales every night. Some of my colleagues said I was stupid, but it's the way I was brought up. In thirty-eight years in the business, I don't know of any instance where I did something to someone that was unfair.

If I shouted at somebody—I have a terrible Irish temper and I'm a very intense person—I would always try to apologize as soon as possible in front of the people who I chewed out. I try to constantly improve myself, but I have a long way to go.

A lot of good came of the pedophile scandal. The inspection for homosexuals in the seminaries was a good thing.

I was in a seminary myself in high school and saw some homosexual influences. The older kids would kind of hang around with the younger kids and treat them as favorites. I didn't really know anything about homosexuality at that time, but I realized later that there must have been some same-sex attraction going on there.

The Church teaches that abortion is always wrong; it's never right to directly kill an innocent person, even if a supposed "good" result is foreseen. In this belief, the Church doesn't say that a baby's life is more important than the mother's, but that they're equal and that one may never directly kill either one of them. I believe in whatever the Church thinks because that's also what God thinks, and who am I to argue with God? Also, there are many stories about wonderful things that've happened to people who were born and were going to be aborted.

With regard to death, I believe what the Church teaches—that our souls live forever; we ultimately either go to heaven or hell. If

I'm lucky I'll go to purgatory, which the Church teaches is a place of purification in preparation for heaven.

Everybody's trying to describe heaven. Maybe they can't because it's beyond description; Christ says it's something so much better than anything we can imagine. I'll accept that, because I'm sure my limited idea of heaven pales in comparison to Christ's heaven. I would be living in a Frank Lloyd Wright house, and I'd have all these virgins in there. God's heaven is a lot more meaningful and joyous than anything I could imagine, so why try to define heaven, because I'm incapable.

Hell is suffering worse than anything we can imagine on this earth. I want to make darn sure I don't wind up there.

If I were pope, I'd be very careful to select faithful bishops, and I'd work to help Catholic education. As far as educating the faithful, I'd probably change some things back to the way they used to be. For example, when the hierarchy changed the obligation of not eating meat on Fridays throughout the year, they said that they encouraged us to still refrain from having meat, but it's not an obligation anymore. I'd change this back, because I think Catholics need some things that remind them that they're Catholics.

A lot of people I know, when they see the words "peace" and "justice," are skeptical. Those programs are often thought of as warm and fuzzy. Almost Protestant. A serious Catholic should be concentrating on saving the soul. I know the Immokalee farmworkers live near our campus. Some people see their mission as doing social justice work. Ours here at Ave Maria is more spiritual. Maybe we can start a program to help save their souls so they'll go to heaven.

Do you go to Mass every Sunday? It's a mortal sin to skip Mass on Sunday without a legitimate reason. You have to go to confession for that. It's another mortal sin to accept the Eucharist if you've committed a mortal sin and not confessed it.

MARY JO BANE

*Mary Jo Bane (b. February 24, 1942) is an academic
dean and professor of public policy and management
at Harvard University's Kennedy School of Government.
She teaches and does research in the areas of public
management, poverty, welfare, and social policy.*

. . . .

My dad worked for the Department of Agriculture as an audi-
tor and he was transferred from place to place, so we moved
around a fair amount when I was a kid—from one working middle-
class neighborhood to another. I was always in parochial schools. My
friends were all Catholic.

At that time a lot of the parishes and schools were ethnically
identifiable, and I received my First Communion in an Italian church.
Since we weren't Italian, this distressed my parents greatly, because
according to them we should've been in a good Irish Catholic parish.

While I was in college at Georgetown between 1959 and 1963,
Vatican II was going on. I remember one time in class, when one of
the theology professors said something like, "When people say they
have intellectual doubts about their faith, what they're really looking for is an excuse to have premarital sex." You know, we probably
were. It was all very dramatic at the time, and I stopped going to
church. My parents said, "If you don't go to church, don't come
home." So I went into the Peace Corps.

I didn't get married until I was thirty-three, but Ken and I
had lived together. When we got married, my mother was very
pleased. She did say to me at one point, "Dear, is he Jewish?" I said
he was, and she sort of nodded her head and said, "Well, he's very
nice."

Now I attend services at the Paulist Center, a little haven for
progressive Catholics; it's very much oriented toward service and social justice. It's a home for the walk for hunger. It's also the place
that would periodically get its hands slapped by the cardinal because
it allowed women to do too many things in the liturgy. It has and
continues to have a vision of a Catholic community that is genuinely

inclusive, respectful of women, and oriented toward social justice and service to the poor parts of the tradition.

You say to yourself, "God wants us to build a kingdom of God on this earth. What would an institution look like that expresses those desires of God for humanity and for the world?" It can't be an institution that isn't oriented to the world and broader and inclusive.

An example of this vision, in its concrete details, is a worship space and a community that's open, that doesn't ask people whether they're gay or not. It doesn't stand up and announce there are rules about who receives communion or not. It's genuinely opening and welcoming and a place where people come together to worship and then go out from worship to bring that vision into the world. This church is a joyful church. It's a vision of an institution that reflects God's love for all of humanity and spreads that into the world.

One thing I've tried to spend a little bit of time thinking about is the way that the Catholic Church historically decided to do its charitable work, through Catholic Charities and social organizations, and to divorce it from parishes. In some ways, that was professionalizing the services, and in some ways it was a strategy for the hierarchy to keep control over it and not have these laywomen running around thinking that they were in charge of this. It seems to me that the model that says, "OK, Catholic Charities does our charitable work, we give them money every so often, and then we don't have to do anything else" is somehow the model that the Institutional Church seems to embody. It gets people off the hook.

When I heard that Ratzinger had been elected pope, I thought, "Oh God, this is a disaster," because here's the head of the Inquisition now becoming the pope. I found his first encyclical remarkable: quite lovely, very thoughtful reflections on love with no anathemas; it's really a celebration of God as love. That's not what I expected. The other part of the encyclical is a reflection on charity in the life of the Church and the really important thing that Benedict says in that part of this encyclical is that word, sacrament, and charity are the three integral parts of the mission of the Church.

Catholicism provides a reliable tradition and a rooted, intellectually structured sense of who we are in this world. God has a purpose for us in this life and on earth. It's the purpose of being the people who do God's work of trying to build the kingdom. It is a sense of security in being part of this tradition that has been important to me.

BETSY PAWLICKI, O.P.

Betsy Pawlicki (b. June 28, 1956) is a Dominican Sister of Sinsinawa, Wisconsin. She is equally as passionate about issues of worker justice as she is about teaching and sharing the faith, particularly through her parish Rite of Christian Initiation for Adults program.

. . . .

I'm a baby boomer from western New York. My family was proud of its Polish heritage and an important part of that heritage was being Catholic. On the high holy days like Christmas, Easter, All Souls', and All Saints', we brought out all the Catholic stuff, all the special prayers, trinkets, beads, and rosaries. In the interim, we weren't necessarily going to church every week—there were four of us under ten years old, no regular babysitter, and a family grocery store that was open on the weekends.

I was a public school kid, so I didn't know any nuns or priests. We attended CCD for First Communion and confirmation. All I remember about CCD is cutting out a lot of felt, making banners, using glue, and coming home with nice little tchotchkes. There was nothing about Catholic doctrine or teaching. In the aftermath of Vatican II, it was all so unsettled and people were trying to come to grips with what all of it meant.

As we got older, my sister got to be a "Jesus freak," and I mean that in an affectionate, sisterly kind of way. Everything was Jesus this, Jesus that, Jesus loves you, and Jesus bumper stickers. She gave me a Bible when I was going away to college, and I thought, "How touching; I would've rather had the money." But I took the Bible with me to school, because it was a present from my sister. Then, during those late-night conversations in the dorm, when you discuss and solve all the world's problems because you're so profound—religion was often one of the topics—I realized I didn't have a whole lot to say. I started to look around.

I checked out nondenominational and Protestant groups and even spent some time in one group that people nowadays would call a cult. I flunked out of that cult when they started asking for money to teach me to speak in tongues and prophesy. I got skeptical.

I spent time with the Protestants, and I was impressed that they knew the books of the Bible. I got into scripture, but after a time I felt like I was outgrowing their fundamentalist approach to scripture. It seemed limiting to me.

I'd been working in higher education administration at Notre Dame when I met my friend and colleague Laurie Brink. She was looking at the convent.

Laurie was my canary. Like the bird they sent down into the coal mines ahead of the miners to test for poisonous gas, she went ahead to explore the potential perils of religious life. She entered. I watched how she came back from those meetings and eventually initiated my own investigation, conversations, and discernment process. I entered the same congregation in 1993.

We both became Dominicans, so the initials after our names are O.P.—the Order of Preachers. As Dominicans, theological study is an integral part of our training.

I was especially intrigued by the Church's teaching on the dignity of work and the rights of workers to collectively organize. Social justice is the practical application of the Gospel.

I practice with a Chicago firm founded by two legendary labor lawyers who are Jewish. I'm the only nun. Our clients are individual employees, unions and their members. A lot of working people are struggling these days. We're plaintiffs' attorneys, so ninety-nine out of a hundred times we're on the side of the angels.

I get paid just like any of the other lawyers. Since I don't currently work for a Catholic organization, I get my check in my name. I deposit the check into our congregation's bank account. And each year we do a budget; the credo is, you put in what you make and ask for what you need. We trust that it's going to work out.

I've been asked, as a woman, how do you grapple with the fact that this institution is in many ways antiwoman? There are days when you are fed up with it all. I try not to minimize the pain, discomfort, and embarrassment that flows from uninformed or misguided stances. Our church teaches that all people, men *and* women, were created in the image and likeness of God. That teaching needs to be taken seri-ously. As a church, we haven't realized the fullness of that teaching yet. As a member of the Order of Preachers, the homily is an impor-tant part of the Mass for me. When it's obvious that the priest pre-pared his homily as he walked to the lectern, that angers me. If men are going to be the only ones to be permitted to preach, then I expect them to prepare to do it well.

I find it difficult to go to masses where there are a number of priests on the altar and no women. It does feel more a power state-ment than a ministry. Those are difficult moments.

I pray for the men who are the senior decision makers in our church—that they will come to recognize and value the voices of all who love and comprise our church. At the same time, I know that ours is a global church comprised of diverse cultures, races, national-ities, and understanding. My views, or the American Church's views, are not necessarily shared by all. I hope that I am humble enough to recognize that I don't have the whole truth and the whole perspec-tive. I guess what's been hard is that there is no room for dialogue on the issues right now; that is particularly painful for me personally. What keeps me going is the richness of the sacraments, just worship-ping in common with the rest of the folks in the pews who struggle too with different things. But they still show up and believe that we are people on a journey and our job and our purpose here is to speak our truth, whatever the circumstances. I believe that one can make a difference even if you cannot see it in your lifetime.

I wouldn't want to be the pope just for a year, so I guess the first thing I would do is extend my reign! What is a year in the life of the Church? That is nothing. If you are going to be a despotic pope, a year will probably do. But I would need a longer period to engage all stakeholders and do some Churchwide catechesis.

Douglas Brinkley

Douglas Brinkley (b. December 14, 1960) is a prolific author and a professor of history at Rice University. The late historian Stephen E. Ambrose once called him "the best of the new generation of American historians." He has written award-winning biographies of Jimmy Carter, Rosa Parks, Henry Ford, James Forrestal, and Dean Acheson. He won the 2007 Robert F. Kennedy Book Award for The Great Deluge: Hurricane Katrina, New Orleans, and the Mississippi Gulf Coast *(2006).*

. . . .

I was born in Atlanta, but my parents are from the North and both of them are Catholics. We were raised Catholic in Atlanta, which was a deeply Protestant community. Our church was St. Anthony's and it was down next to the original Krispy Kreme doughnut shop and the Wren's Nest, where Joel Chandler Harris—who wrote the Brer Rabbit stories—used to live. We used to go to Mass all the time, and I looked forward to church because of the doughnuts.

I was in an all-Protestant elementary school with only a handful of Catholics. Back then, there was a feeling of being different—the very fact that our church didn't have the mowed lawns and steeples of the Presbyterian churches or the ornate stone of Episcopalian churches. St. Anthony's was deeply urban. There was an ethereal feel in the church, going through all the rituals that you do of just preparing to be an altar boy.

We moved to Perrysburg, Ohio, when I was eight. I joined St. Rose Church, through Communion and confirmation. What started dawning on me was that you gained a Catholic identity whether you wanted it or not. It's almost like you're all going on a ship and there's a sign saying, "Catholics this way, Protestants this way." You'd start knowing other Catholics in the community, because you'd see each other at Bible classes, Sunday school, or Mass.

Catholicism, to me, is centered on the concept of forgiveness—the notion that I could sin, then have them washed away at confession on Saturday, go to church on Sunday, and have a new slate for the beginning of the week. I found that very convenient, because any kind of crazy boy behavior that I did during the week, I felt I could get absolution for on the weekend. That part of Catholicism has stayed with me. I'll still go to confession or, if not, I pray, say Hail Marys, Our Fathers, and all. Confession helps me feel like I can make up for my mistakes in life—that each day is a new day in that I don't have to carry the baggage of my mistakes for eternity.

I'm one of those American Catholics who has come through Catholicism fairly grateful about it, because the Church has never thrown me a curveball. I disagree with half of the protocol of the Church and with the Vatican. I don't have a sense of following Church doctrine. I'm a lapsed Catholic, but still I look forward to Christmas Eve. My highlight living in New Orleans has been going to Our Lady of Guadalupe's midnight Mass where Aaron Neville sings "Ave Maria." I get excited eight months in advance to go to Mass, and I like going for Palm Sunday, for Easter, or Ash Wednesday. I may be a lapsed Catholic, but I have no desire to give up my Catholicism.

There are aspects of studying the saints, and with the candles, and with incense, and with Latin masses and some of the pageantry of the Church, as an American historian, that make me feel part of a larger wave of history. That it's not a newfangled religion, which some people get great solace from. I feel that I'm connected to places.

Every time I'm about to leave a Catholic church I still find myself able to feel God by going to a pew in an empty church. It's not even the ritual of the Mass so much. I pop into different Catholic churches everywhere I go. You can always duck into a church if it's open, like St. Patrick's, and just say a prayer for somebody. I've always believed there's some power in prayer. At times it's worked for me and the Catholic Church is a facilitator for that.

I did my master's and doctorate at Georgetown with the Jesuits and some of my best teachers have been Catholic priests.

When you talk about the founding fathers, none of them were Catholics. They were all Masons and the Masonic temples wouldn't allow Catholics to join. The person whom American Catholics had to turn to is Christopher Columbus, who is no longer a sustainable hero.

Catholics have been ostracized for a long time, like African Americans, Jews, or other minority groups, so there's a bit of an outcast status about being Catholic that I think still exists.

Today, you have a quarter of Americans that are Catholic. It's an immense power base, and yet it doesn't always operate in a unified way. Today, politically in America, Catholicism is in disarray.

I edited all of Jack Kerouac's diaries in a book called *Wind Blown World* and Kerouac was deeply Catholic. Catholicism exuded out of his work, and when you read his diaries, he's always looking to God for forgiveness, looking after the meek, and looking after the Lamb of God who are the people you can help the most. It's about having a conscience, about keeping your spirit open. He was one of those writers that if he saw a guy with no legs sitting on the street with a tin cup, Kerouac would sit down and say, "Tell me your story." He recognized that you need to stop and look at those we normally walk past, that they're not invisible, and that each of them has this great story. As a writer, that aspect of Kerouac appeals to me.

It's not a matter of just giving them a dollar to put my conscience to the test, but I try to look them in the eyes, because I don't like myself if I act like they don't exist. You're torn, because you don't want to get into a thing with someone who seems unstable, but I remember Kerouac talking about how important it was to do that for your own self. This concept of charity that's in Catholicism infused his best books.

I read an article in the *New York Times* about a man named Father Michael McGivney, how the Vatican was considering him for sainthood, and how he created the Knights of Columbus. What McGivney said is, as Catholics, we've got to put America first and Catholicism second. We've got to convince Protestant culture that we're not in some secret alliance with the Vatican. We need to be public. He created Catholic-forward bake sales, sponsored baseball in the park, and produced plays to present Catholics as community people.

It used to be the highest calling of a Catholic family to have one member of the family who became a priest. That was who they were most proud of. We don't have that anymore today. And it's because of problems in Church politics, corruption, and pedophilia.

I felt when I wrote *Parish Priest* that I was seeing the whole concept of priesthood in America disintegrating. I'm a bleeding heart, so I started feeling bad for all these priests who I knew were really great people who were being laughed at now. They never did anything wrong, but because there were some priests who were so terrible, the whole concept of being a priest was under suspicion.

I'd never write a book on a pope, bishop, or cardinal, because I'm totally uninterested in Catholic hierarchy, but what I'm interested in is that there are a lot of really great priests who I've had as teachers, who I've seen help people when they were in despair, and those people need to be thanked by our society.

Somehow, when you're raised Catholic, it's brought into you. I get very guilty if I feel like I've maligned somebody, because naturally we talk and have loose lips. You try not to carry around hatred with you. You try to talk more positively about people. We fail at that all the time.

I don't go to confession regularly. I go about fifteen or twenty times a year. I go to Mass, but I miss a lot. I go to the shortest Mass possible. It's at seven o'clock at night and I have a huge dinner afterward with friends. I feel like I can say a few prayers. When they say, "Peace be with you," and you shake people's hands, it's kind of nice to get to say hi to some people. I've never walked out of church feeling bad.

In church I think about something I want to do better, something I did wrong, or ask God to forgive me for something I may've done. I'm not there for the religiosity so much as a form of meditation, a place just to say a prayer, to say hi to some people, and to get my alignment right.

I don't consider myself an activist, but I think it's essential that people have the opportunity to pray when they or someone else is sick or dying.

My mind prays every forty-eight hours. I don't go on my hands and knees like a cartoon. To me, prayer is a mental reflection on just how lucky I am to be able to walk and breathe. I don't want to take life for granted.

I like to take a time-out and say, oh my God, I met that guy who had no legs or I met that woman who just lost her husband and they're in such pain right now and what kind of punk am I to be whining about myself because I'm in bumper-to-bumper traffic in my SUV. That's when I say a prayer. I use it to pull me back a little, recognize that I've been given gifts and blessings and to not take them for granted. Prayer is a way to even the playing field a little.

I think the basic line is that you know when you're doing something evil and it's not a matter of sinning. People who sin all the time can also be heroes. I saw that during Katrina, a lot of downcast people with prison records and people of a criminal class were saving people's lives and risking their lives by jumping into the stagnant water helping people. In our heads we know what's positive and what's negative. There is something that's going on that's bigger than we know and somehow you know inside what's the right thing to do and the wrong thing. It's about kindness.

I don't believe in a place called heaven where we're all going to be congregating, but I do believe after talking to enough people that you do get an out-of-body experience—that you have a soul, which is different from the body. I do think it goes somewhere, because if you've ever had an out-of-body experience, you can feel that whatever's in you is different from the body. It's that energy of who you are. Perhaps there is reincarnation. Regardless, where our soul goes is the great mystery. The most I'd tell people who are struggling with disbelief is having faith doesn't hurt.

I'm terrified of death, because I love life so much. I guess part of Catholicism is telling people that you live on. Maybe when I'm getting near death, I'll find solace in that. I don't want to believe that you're just in the ground; it means nothing. I like to think there's still a journey.

If I were pope for a year I'd try to redirect the Catholic Church away from the political realm and more on a grassroots of helping people. I'd support dealing with the world, with poverty that's so rampant. I'd focus on the people in need around the world and on human rights issues, not these kinds of traditionalist notions.

One of the last things I'd say is that the power of the crucifixion of Christ, the way Catholics display his death in statues, always kind of haunts me. Protestants have more modern crosses but when you go in these Catholic churches, you go through the stations of the cross. That had a dramatic effect on me as a child, of suffering, and whenever you're in a situation when you're ill or you're in a kind of pain, if you flash back, you won't hear a more horrific story than the crucifixion story of Christ. It infuses your thinking a lot because there's the thought that there was a resurrection from all of that. That even maybe when your life is so down and bad that maybe there's something better coming.

When you hit forty, you get to know who you are, and instead of running from it, I've embraced it a little more. It's part of me. I don't know why I do have Catholic guilt. They rammed it into me somehow. I don't want to spend my life trying to deconstruct myself. I'm more "Ah, that's who I am." There are worse things for me to have than some Catholic guilt. There are worse things than learning to pray. I don't need to get rid of it, because I don't really have anything to turn to. If I did it'd be Buddhism, and that takes time, and the more I read about Buddhism, I like a lot about it, but I don't have the time to invest in it whereas Catholicism is like putting on my wingtips and going to church.

GAY TALESE

Gay Talese (b. February 7, 1932) is the bestselling author of eleven books, whose writing style broke new ground in literary nonfiction. Talese's 1966 Esquire *article, "Frank Sinatra Has a Cold," is one of the most influential American magazine articles of all time, inspiring magazine editors to accept his technique of writing about the creating and compiling of the story itself, rather than simply writing about the subject. He rose to become one of the country's foremost essayists and a leading practitioner of New Journalism.*

. . . .

"Beginnings"

I am seventy-six. I was born in February 1932 of Italian Catholics in Ocean City, New Jersey, near Atlantic City. And this town, settled by Methodist ministers in the 1870s, was a Protestant island. In the summertime there must have been nearly seventy thousand people; I'm speaking of the 1930s and 1940s in the World War II years. But in the wintertime, the island population shrunk to about six thousand, of which I would bet fifty-five hundred were Protestants, not just Methodists but Episcopalians and everything else.

There was a minority Catholic parish, which had probably three hundred parishioners, of which there was a very small group of about a dozen or so Italians. Italians built the railroad attaching Ocean City to Atlantic City and then Philadelphia in the 1880s. And some of them stayed.

My father was a tailor, born in Italy in 1903. He worked with uncles who were tailors in Paris, then came to America in 1920 and went to Philadelphia. He was a Catholic and in 1922 settled in Ocean City. He lived as a bachelor for about eight years there and had a tailor shop catering to the Methodist elite. They were the lawyers, the bankers, the ministers, whoever passed for the establishment on this sandy shore. But he was a Catholic and he attended Mass regularly.

The Ku Klux Klan burned a cross in Ocean City in the early 1920s, directed at the Catholics, and I saw men in sheets when I was a kid. You don't have to go to Birmingham for this. The leading pharmacist in our town was the head of this Klan, but he was a man who graduated from the Philadelphia College of Pharmacy and he had a sense of presence about him that gave you the impression he was a gentleman—very rigid, but in his secret private life, in the dark shadows of his white shirt, he was a lurking Klansman. There's a lot of hypocrisy in small towns that is evident and pervasive.

St. Augustine's was a church, which, on weekdays, had bamboo rollers that came from the ceiling to the floor, rolling off and forming a classroom. That's where I went to school, grades one to eight. On Saturdays, when confessions were heard, and on Sundays, when Mass was said, the rollers were moved up to the ceiling. We were taught by nuns, some of them born in Ireland, and I was the Italian altar boy. When I reached the age of fourteen, I went to the public school in town, Ocean City High School, and then to the University of Alabama.

I was a very fearful Catholic. The Church—or at least the parish that I was influenced by—prepared you for death. There was a sense that you'd better be prepared, because without warning you could die and you would go to hell, burning forever.

This has left a mark on me to this day; it shapes my work. When I was a reporter for the *New York Times*, it was a governing factor. There was this fear of making mistakes—don't be careless, you will be punished, nothing is guaranteed, don't believe in anything until you see it—a sense of caution and concern that I would be in error or in a compromising position or a sinner of some sort. When you're an immigrant, a son of outsiders, you don't want to do anything to discredit them because they're insecure enough and they're trying to rise socially. If you are the offspring of such an arrangement of such a couple whose sense of virtue is probably more pronounced than it should be, you become careful.

My father was always elegantly dressed like I am. My mother has a dress shop; she was very slender and I thought I had the best-looking mother in town. She was born in Brooklyn's white Italian ghetto, and then she went to work for a large department store. She got to know a lot of people who were not like those in her neighborhood, and she got to know fashion and perfume. When you do that, you are elevated from your insularity as an ethnic. Once she moved out of Brooklyn, she rarely ever returned, because she also wanted to separate herself from the ghetto. So my father was from Calabria,

Italy, with his suits, and my mother with her dress shop, having learned about fashion from the largest shop in Brooklyn, started a life together of assimilation if not social acceptance. And when you grow up with awareness, you, too, become careful and polite.

Catholicism wasn't something I could get away from, because it was overwhelming in my altar boy days and during my high school years. I joined the Newman Club in college in 1949, when I was seventeen, and gradually shifted away, but not so much in the spiritual sense. I was a thousand miles from home, and no one knew anything about me. I was allowed to start again; it was my second chance.

I met my future wife, Nan, in 1957, four years after graduation from college, and I'd just started my career with the *New York Times*. Nan and I married outside the Church. I really didn't care about her religion; it was totally accidental that I would be comfortable with a woman with a Catholic education and, in fact, a rather elitist one. Certainly in a class sense I was marrying up. Her father married a woman twenty-two years his junior, who converted to Catholicism. Her father, a corporate lawyer and fund-raiser for worthy causes, was not a teetotaler.

Not long after I met Nan, we became enamored of each other and got sexually involved after a year. I went to Rye to meet her parents a couple of times during the premarital period, and a lot of Nan's friends from the clubs felt that she was marrying the wrong kind. I was outside of the tracks, and I picked up on that. It suddenly threw me right back to my early feeling in Ocean City.

Her mother did not want her to go out with me. She had ambitions for her daughter. Nan was the prettiest of the girls, and her mother had high hopes for her socially. Nan wanted to get out of there. And even though I wasn't the dream candidate and she was dating other people, for some reason—maybe a bit of rebellion—she became attached to me. I did not want to go back to Rye anymore.

I was looked upon as an outsider and I no longer wanted to feel like one. Nan wanted to be with me, she said. But we couldn't just live together in those days. I simply didn't know what to do. But

Nan said her mother wanted us to get married in church. We had to get married.

In 1959 I got an assignment to go to Rome to write an article for the *New York Times Magazine* on Federico Fellini, who was making *La Dolce Vita*, but I was actually writing about the city of Rome and the main street, and that's when I called Nan and said to come over. We essentially eloped. She called her parents and said she was going to go. Her father said, go ahead. Her mother said, get married in church—in the Trinità dei Monti. But they no longer had weddings in that church, and we finally ended up in a civil ceremony in a beautiful place. Nan's mother was furious; she said, "I will never talk to you." I said, "I will not speak to you, either." And we didn't for about thirty-five years.

Even though it's been a long time since I've been a churchgoer, there are certain Catholic principles that affect me to this day—a sense of honor and a sense of truth. It would help if some of today's journalists really believed that, as I believe it. I got that from the nuns, echoed by the priests—the fact that what matters is not just today; there's a longer measure, a greater life out there. It's a life hereafter.

George Eliot writes about how religion is a fear of the hereafter. People need religion, because they have to have some belief in that they're not just going to perish, that it matters that a lifetime of dedication to certain standards will pay off, otherwise why bother? It doesn't end with your heart ceasing to be. It goes on and on. I believe that. What I do is going to be measured long after I'm dead. That is what I carried of Catholicism, so in a religious sense, I do have a sense of religiosity inculcated in the work I do and the attitude I have about work.

I don't go to Mass now, but I do pray. It's a cliché—once a Catholic, always a Catholic. You don't convert to anything else.

And yet with me, there are certain areas of Catholic teachings that don't have a hold. While I've had lust in my heart—like Jimmy Carter—I've never wanted to leave my wife for another woman. But

I have women friends who've been friends of mine for twenty-five to thirty years. They're like an adjunct of my marriage. My marriage is here, my children are here, and I may have a lady friend in Alabama who goes back to my college days, or someone I met in Los Angeles in 1976, or China. I have these people in my life that I write to, call, and care about.

I would see my mother, who died last August, and my father, who died in 1993, twice a week. This is the type of thing that I got out of what I thought was Catholicism—the idea of being responsible. There is a certain respect you pay, and not only out of a sense of obligation. There are things you're supposed to do. I measure friendship by how willing people are to be inconvenienced by the friendship. It's a test. It's very easy to be a friend of somebody important, but what happens when a person is down and out, has lost the talk show, is no longer a book editor, or no longer has a potential use to you?

We've been going to funerals lately, because many of my friends are dying. One of them we went to recently was Gordon Parks, and in the cab coming back we were talking about our funerals. We decided that we should have our funerals in church, but what church? We haven't been to church. I'm now going to have to cultivate a relationship with the pastor. That's Catholicism. I haven't been in church in fifty years, but now I have to deal with the Maker and also have a nice reception. We now have to lay the groundwork with the proper donations.

I may not be entirely formed, but I was greatly influenced by my Catholic upbringing. And that is, you can't escape responsibility; you're going to be found out. Better to do good work that matters.

STEVEN OTELLINI

Steven Otellini (b. April 28, 1952) is Monsignor at the Church of the Nativity in Menlo Park, California. He served on the Vatican Diplomatic Corps as assistant to the Papal Nuncio to the Central African Republic, Chad, the Congo, and later in Greece.

. . . .

I was born and raised in San Francisco. I'm in the second generation of American citizens. My mother still lives in the house that
my parents bought right after they were married, an indication of
the remarkable stability in which I was raised. San Francisco was
very different than it is now. I went to Catholic grammar school, and
by eighth grade I had a strong enough inclination to join the priesthood that I enrolled in the seminary.

Becoming a priest isn't something I chose to do; rather, it's a vocation, and I chose to respond to the call. The question is, do I have
the ability to respond to it and be faithful to it? There were difficult
times in the Church. I entered in 1966, so the Vatican Council had
just ended and all of the changes—not just the liturgical changes
but the sociological and theological changes—were going on and it
was a whirlwind of activity inside and outside the seminary.

After I finished my license degree, the bishop asked me to return
to Rome to do studies for the diplomatic service.

When I was told my first assignment would be Bangui, I went to
my friend E. J. Dionne, who covered the Vatican and had gone there
with the pope. "So," I said, "what is in Bangui?" And he said, "There
is a lovely hotel that has a kind of a terrace that overlooks nothing of
downtown Bangui."

After Africa, I went to Greece. Then I came back to pastoral du-
ties in San Francisco before the bishop assigned me to be president of
Marin High School.

The phenomenon of Catholic education in the United States
dramatically changed American society over the past hundred years.
The vast majority of Italian immigrants in the United States had no
education whatsoever. Two generations after the first real wave of
Italian immigration you look at the proportion of people who have

achieved higher degrees or made contributions in business or science and there is a huge proportion of those who are Italian Catholics. So here, from a noneducated group who primarily were educated in Catholic grammar school systems, now we have Antonin Scalia sitting on the Supreme Court; it is an extraordinary thing.

The future is bright, but there is a growing danger of elitism attached to it, primarily because of expenses. To maintain a quality faculty you want to pay them a somewhat decent salary and obviously we were getting no government aid and had no endowment. When I left, tuition was twelve thousand dollars a year, which is pretty steep for a new immigrant. At Marin, 80 percent of the kids were Catholic, and of those who were not Catholic, almost all of the others were Christians, a few Muslims, and maybe one or two Jewish boys.

Aside from the very important role of communicating a Catholic formation to people, which is the reason for our existence, the secondary benefit we're giving these people is a quality education and a head start for their lives.

When we're children, we picture ourselves sitting with the angels in the company of friends in heaven. As we mature and our faith grows, we begin to learn that heaven is going to be a fuller, more complete experience of the life in the world as we see it now, with all of those anxieties, tensions, and limitedness that we experience here removed.

It isn't the case that people who go to hell cease to be loved by God, but they've been placed in hell by ceasing to love in a way in which Christ teaches us to love God and our neighbor.

Heaven isn't like Disneyland, where once you get through the gate you get to go on the rides for free. The idea is that we make ourselves capable of receiving God's love in this world. And, to the extent that we make ourselves receptive to God's love, God will fill that up in us. So that is very different for each human being. To the extent that we have done away with our selfishness in this world and opened ourselves to God's love, then in heaven, we will be filled. It is going to be different for someone who has lived a very selfless life and someone who has lived a somewhat selfish life than for those who have opened themselves up only a little bit.

The spiritual enjoyment of someone like St. Francis of Assisi or Mother Teresa is going to be much greater than someone who—in the last minute—decided that their life was kind of miserable and they did convert and turned to the Lord and made their act of contrition and died. Their enjoyment of God and their capacity to receive God is probably very small compared to these great saints and therefore God will fill up certainly what is there, but it is going to be different in both of those cases.

MARTIN SHEEN

*Martin Sheen (né Ramón Estévez, August 3, 1940) is a
three-time Emmy and Golden Globe Award—winning actor,
best known for his roles in the film* Apocalypse Now *and
the television drama series* The West Wing. *Sheen is a
devoted Catholic known for his robust support of liberal
political causes. He has advocated for a wide range of
human rights, peace, and environmental causes, particularly
focused on immigrants' rights and antipoverty issues.*

*Sheen is shown above at his First Communion in
Dayton, Ohio.*

. . . .

Both of my parents were very devout Catholics from Spain and Ireland. I grew up in a large family: nine boys and one girl. My mother died when I was about eleven. So I grew up in a very traditional, immigrant type of Catholic family, first-generation Americans. I was educated in grade school by the Sisters of Notre Dame, and then went to an all-boys Catholic high school.

I was an altar boy in the Old Latin Church, a lot of which I still remember. I drifted from the Church and the faith for a long time, starting in the early 1960s, right when it was changing. I was focused on a career, we were starting our family; every now and then I'd go to Mass or confession, but I really wasn't steady.

Catholicism didn't have a personal meaning to me until 1977, when I had a heart attack in the Philippines while working on *Apocalypse Now* and that woke me up. I had the last rites, and when I recovered, I became very devout again. Then I realized my devotion was out of fear of dying and going to the other side unprepared, and I wanted to be on the winning side! Eventually, I let it go again; I was drinking very heavily. I'm a known alcoholic.

I was on a search that culminated in India in 1981. I went there to do a small part in the movie *Gandhi*. I'd been in third-world countries before, but I'd never seen that depth of human poverty and degradation. It made a profound impression on me.

From there I went to Paris for three months, and I had a lot of time to reflect on what I'd seen in India and the path that I'd been on for all of these years, particularly the last four. I was staying in a hotel across from St. Joseph's Church in Paris, and it was the only English-speaking church in all of France. I dropped in and I was somewhat astonished that it was all in English. How extraordinary: The priest was facing the people; now I started to get interested.

An old dear friend of my mine—Terry Malick, the director of *Badlands*—was living in Paris, and I ran into him by accident on the street one day. We were both living on the Left Bank, and he was a very devout and deeply spiritual man, less religious than spiritual but very religious too. He became, not by either of our choices, but just by reality, a spiritual adviser for me and my confidant. I began to tell him about my search, and he would give me literature to read. We'd go to services sometimes.

The last book he gave to me was *The Brothers Karamazov* and that had a profound effect on me. I was so moved by how an artist could speak to the problems of the heart, the soul, and the spirit. That was the step that I knew I needed to take.

I had May 1, 1981, off. In Europe, of course, it was a national holiday. So I went to church. It was one of those days when you wake up and know this is the day you have to do this and nothing is going to deter you. I decided I would come back to the Church.

I went to church and the door was locked. I was knocking and ringing the bell. I waited and waited and nobody came. I pounded and pounded. I thought, "Am I meant to do this?" I felt that the impetus was there. And then I thought maybe it wasn't meant to be. I pounded again and finally I gave up. Just as I came down the steps, the doors flew open. The priest was standing there eating his lunch, and he had some food on his face and a napkin in his hand. He looked over the top of my head as if there was an emergency, because of all the banging and ringing. He looked down at me and said, "What is it?" I said, "I'm sorry to bother you, Father, but I've been away from the Church many, many years and I'd like to come back. I'd like to go to confession."

He looked at me and something behind his eyes said, "You came to the right place." He knew that it was an important moment for me; he got it instantly. It was the most extraordinary confession. All of my brokenness poured out and he said, "Welcome back." I was so overjoyed and that started the honeymoon. I'd come back out of love and joy, no longer fear; it was mine now. I wasn't afraid of dying; I was afraid of not living, not really being alive.

It's got to be personal and until 1981 it was never personal with me. It was always something that was given to me, and I felt that I had to do it. I had to be a Catholic and do all things righteously, because if you didn't you will go to hell. God forbid.

I don't know what salvation means in a personal sense. For me, a better word is "freedom." We're meant to be free, spiritually, emotionally, and physically; we have to know we're human. I don't think we can ever be talked out of that once we're anchored in a faith, once we're able to see God's presence. The central mystery of Catholicism is so powerful. It's simple. God becomes human. Go figure.

I was almost forty-one years old before I had a sense of being loved. If your religion isn't about truly being loved, I don't know if you can translate it into daily life. You have to know it if you're loved.

I'm still like a child when I get on line for Communion. I have a little prayer I say just to get me to that place of reception: "I'm Ramón, called Martin, your brother, you are welcome here. Whatever you bring is a feeling of absolute freedom and joy."

I had a whole bunch of arrests during the wars in El Salvador and Nicaragua. We had a coalition. We would get arrested every Wednesday morning. I would spend a day in jail and then have to appear in front of a judge. It is a federal thing. I came before this wonderful woman judge. I had like a dozen or more arrests at that point. I am always arrested under my real name, Ramón. So she said, "Ramón, what am I going to do with you?" She was shaking her head and said, "It doesn't do anything to send you to jail; you will go there every week. Will you give community service?" I said, "I will." Since it didn't have any impact to send me to jail, the judge gave me community service in a soup kitchen run by Sister Rose Herrington, one of my heroes. Sister Rose said, "Will you wash dishes?" I said I could. She explained that they called clients Ma'am and Sir. They were always kind and courteous to clients and if you came there to help, you were privileged to serve these people.

I stayed ten years because I loved it.

One day a very fundamentalist fellow came in. I don't know what religion he was; he could have even been Catholic. He thought we should have grace before meals with the homeless and he approached the Sister about it. Sister said, "The grace is that we're given this privilege to serve them. I don't think we have to trouble them with religion." She was made free by the work.

Most Christian religions in America are very convenient. There's this sense of, all I have to do is this, this, and this. You're not being challenged, and no one's going to insist that you step up. A long time ago, I got used to not being comfortable. I'm never as comfortable as when I'm uncomfortable. It's true spiritually; it's that I always have a sense of choice in this matter. The choice is always human. When it's not human I feel concerned.

Mother Teresa said it was easier to deal with the worst poverty in the third world than it was to deal with the absence of spirituality in America. It was like we were struggling with our possessions, with our image, with our comfort, really, and that was more painful for her.

I have a dear friend, Joe Cosgrove; he's the lawyer who represents me in criminal cases. He called me up during the first Gulf War and asked if I was free to join him on a peace mission to Rome to meet up with Mother Teresa.

I went over to New York and met him at the airport and he said, "It's just you and me." I said, "Are you nuts? We're on a peace mission to stop the war? Just you and me? What's your plan?" He said, "Mother is going to meet us when we get there. I've drawn up a writ to represent the Vatican at the World Court in The Hague, because the only nation to oppose the war unilaterally and ask for coming together is the Vatican. I'm having trouble getting through to get permission from the pope, and I'm going to explain my position. Mother is going to see the Holy Father the next day and if she agrees with this writ she'll put in a word for us. Then I'll go to The Hague and represent the Vatican."

We got to Rome, we went into this chapel, and as Sister came and said, "Mother will receive you," the door burst open and she came in. I wept. We stood up and she was tiny; she was as small as a child. I thought she was eight feet tall, what was she doing being a child?

She was full of energy. Joe went about explaining his motivations, and I was sitting there with my mouth open. Mother was listening to every word. And she said, "You want to represent the Vatican at the World Court?" Joe said, "That's my intention." She said, "Sounds like a wonderful idea; you want me to take this to the pope? Yes, I will do that."

She asked about our families and what we did with our lives. Joe said he was defending people on death row primarily; he was a public defender. He lived like a monk; he was still paying his student loans to Notre Dame, and he was almost fifty years old. He didn't have a clue that he was poor.

At one point, she was seated between us at the card table, and she was getting into a very interesting discussion with Joe. She was reminding him, as if he needed to be reminded, how everything he does is related to God, that no human being is without the divine presence. She reached out, took his hand, placed it on the table, flattened it, and then she said, one word at a time, while touching each finger in succession, "You did it to me." Now I'm looking at that scene and I'm jealous. Mother Teresa is blessing him with all these things, and he's getting all the attention, when suddenly, she reached over and took my hand, placed it on the table, then placed hers firmly over mine. And I thought, "Don't mess with this woman."

We were there for over an hour with her. It was the most extraordinary time, and then she bid us good night and she went to the Vatican the next day. Joe and I hung around, and then Friday morning we came to the early English-speaking Mass. When we got there it was enough; the war had ended that morning. It was February 1991, and Joe said, "Don't mess with Mother Teresa."

During the Mass, we were all crowded in this tiny place. There must have been a hundred people in there, all American, mostly

English speaking, and when we got to intentions, everybody got their licks in "for my uncle so and so . . . Lord hear our prayers." Then it got real quiet. And this voice said, "Let us remember to pray for all those we promised to pray for." And that was Mother.

She had a very profound effect on me, and all of us.

PEGGY NOONAN

Peggy Noonan (b. September 7, 1950) is the author of seven books on politics, religion, and culture, five of which have been New York Times *bestsellers. She was a special assistant to President Ronald Reagan, working with him on some of his most well-known speeches, and a chief speechwriter for Vice President George H. W. Bush when he ran for president in 1988. Noonan's writings are informed by a working-class, populist sympathy, a conservative perspective, and a Roman Catholic spirituality.*

. . . .

I'm the grandchild of Irish immigrants. My grandparents, great-aunts, and great-uncles were schooled in Irish Catholicism. Not all of them went to church, but one who did was my great-aunt Mary Jane. She never said, "This is what you think; this is what you do." She just took me to church. She had prayer cards in her mirror. If you walked into her bedroom, there were rosary beads on the bedside table. She made a big impression on me.

My parents weren't particularly interested in the Church and didn't really like it. They were culturally Catholic but not practitioners of their religion. However, on Sundays they'd say, "Go to church."

I'm the third of seven kids. My childhood was pretty chaotic. Churches were peaceful, tall, dark, old, quiet, reflective places of profound equality. You are taught as a Catholic that nobody's better than anybody else. We're all children of God. I was drawn to the implicit equality.

I always tell priests, "Have real candles; don't get those little electrical things with the button you push." You smell that smell, and it's obviously an olfactory sensation, but it's one of the ways you sense you're home. You can sit by yourself and talk to God, and he probably won't bop you on the head.

I became a *true* Catholic at age forty. I always felt the tug of my religion, my faith, but I'd swim in and out of connection for many years. In some ways, it was so strongly in me, but in many ways it wasn't convenient to live a Catholic life, or to come back to basics.

Then when I was forty, suddenly I knew that I needed Christ. I felt empty in my life. I knew loads of people who were religious, which isn't necessarily usual—at least in New York. Most of them were various kinds of Bible-group-going or evangelical Protestants.

When I would talk to them and say, "I feel like I'm thirsting for something," they'd say, "It's for Jesus, come to Bible school." These people urged me to read the Bible for the first time in my life. I owe them a lot. I'll never forget sitting in my apartment reading Acts of the Apostles one morning. I realized this is the story of the apostles after Jesus died and rose. This is a fabulous story! So, all those wonderful people were certain that they were helping me to become an evangelical Protestant. Well, ironically, what they helped me to become was a real Catholic. It was a great experience for me to be brought back to Christ by Protestants. It gave me an admiration for them and their lovely personal relationship with Christ.

Catholicism was in my bones. Everything I've ever read that was Catholic was true to me. I just got it.

At the time, I had great recent success and the destabilization of that. That can be a real drama in your life, very much, as much as real failure—divorce, confusion, trying to bring my son up by myself when I didn't know exactly how to. All of these things were real crises for me. Not knowing what my future was. Not knowing how I could support myself.

I have a very small and a very easy Catholic school class that I teach once a week and we've been talking about guardian angels recently. I told the girls this story. We'd had a small meeting of the teachers of the Catholic instruction class, and one of the teachers, an elderly lady, at this get-to-know-each-other thing, started chatting with me, and she started talking about her guardian angel. It was so cute and so touching. From out of nowhere, she said, "Do you believe in guardian angels?" I said, "Yeah, I do; I think we all have one." She said, "Do you ever imagine how yours looks?" I said, "No, not really," and she said she had imagined what hers looked like and had also asked to find out its name. She prayed on it for months: "Let me know your name." Then she was walking down the stairs in her empty home one day and suddenly she heard the words. I cannot remember the name, but it was something like "I'm Michael." And she thought, "Michael, who's that? What an odd thing." She got in the car, rode on, and realized why she'd heard those words. "I know what that was." It was an answer to her prayers. I love simple belief if it is true, simple belief that is not just another form of silliness. I do believe these things are true, and I loved her unselfconscious speaking of angels. The girls in my class like the story.

Saying the Rosary helps you; saying prayer after prayer, linking them together, can help your mind reflect and go places. It almost summons God and makes him help you. I think he likes it when you just talk to him, too. I'm a big believer in "God, I'm having a good moment, thank you for this," and then just keep going.

I think about God a lot. I try to wake up with a prayer. This is very recent for me. A friend of mine convinced me that you ought to, as soon as you get out of bed in the morning, say a prayer and give God the day. Just sanctify the day to God. Give him your joys and sorrows, your efforts, your work, your disappointments, and your real pleasure walking down the street. Give it to him and ask him to do with it what he needs and what he must. That's probably my most important prayer. I have a feeling it would be everybody's most important prayer if they did it.

George Bush is said to start out his day with Bible reading. I was on a plane recently, and I brought with me a book on how the biggest problem for man on earth is that he doesn't believe enough in God or trust in him. It said, if you trust God you'll be happy because you can hand over your white-knuckled fear to him; you put everything in his hands. The interesting thing about faith and Christ is that you never get it; it's constant thinking, discovering, making new connections, concluding, and learning.

The Bible is still the great book. I'm into the lives of the saints lately. I love their doubts and their struggles. One of my favorite books is *Saints for Sinners*. It's about more or less obscure, deeply imperfect people who were great. They're killer saints, soldier saints, whore saints, and liar saints. People who found out what was true and it changed their lives.

So many of the modern iterations of the Bible are graceless, and it bugs me. I heard the Twenty-third Psalm recently, and they changed "He leadeth me to green pastures" to "He takes me to a verdant place." They make it harder for you to believe by clunking up the language and depoetizing it. All little kids get what "my cup runneth over" means. "You make my drinking vessel overflow" is something that would only bore them. It sounds like a plumber. I have to make out a will saying, "Please say certain prayers at my funeral, not the newfangled version—the oldfangled." We should all watch out for that or else we'll wind up with some guy saying, "He takes me to the verdant place where the vessel overflows." Those who took the simplicity and poetry from the Bible and from the catechism did a rather wicked thing. I hope it wasn't deliberate.

Because of these and of our own changes it's going to be harder for the next generation to maintain Catholic tradition. Our parents grew up in an America that assumed church as a reality, and our kids are growing up in a post-church America. I try to pass on the essentials: Jesus is real; God is real. The most real sentence you'll ever hear is "Christ was born, lived, died for me and was resurrected." Everything else will come and go. The fabulous jacket you just got, the ratings on the show that you love—everything comes and goes. That doesn't come and go. It's real and it's forever. I raised my son within the Church, but I'm utterly aware and accepting of the fact that he's an independent young man who will go and figure it out on his own. I also believe, since I pray about him a lot, that he'll be fine and find the truth.

I don't disagree with any of the teachings of the Catholic Church. Pope Benedict had his big statement on Islam and Christianity recently, and as far as I'm concerned, everybody can argue about that and say he is wrong or right. There will always be a left, right, and a center, or a "this club" and "that club," but if we keep our eyes on the essentials, we'll stick together, stay together, and move forward. We had better do that because it's a rough old world. I worry that the Church is becoming divided between theological conservatives and liberals. I don't like it, and I want us to all work together more. We're

Catholics and that is enough to unite Catholic Republicans and Catholic Democrats. And then we can differ on political policy stuff. If you're Catholic, you care about the poor and it's where your sympathies are and your heart is, but you can come to very different policy thoughts about how to help. At least we're all starting at the same place. I wouldn't have advice for a friend who disagrees with the Church. I know doctrine is a struggle for modern Catholics, but I think it's always been a struggle for all Catholics. It's not for sissies. Part of me thinks, "Could we leave this to the theologians?" Let them figure it out, and I'll keep my eyes on the prize. To keep my eyes on the central truth. I try not to ever argue with people about these things that are, at the bottom, mysterious. I bring a very grateful heart to Catholicism. Probably most of the great saints brought a fighting or turbulent heart. I'm one of the people who wants to say, in part, go figure it out and let me know. I know that what I'm saying is wrong in a way, and I know it's at odds with the spirit of the age. However, that's where I am.

I never thought about birth control much until I saw Mother Teresa speak about it in Washington. She spoke of abortion and artificial forms of contraception, and where the Church stands and why. For the first time, I thought, "I understand." She put it in terms of love, honoring each other, and honoring God. It makes me uncomfortable because I have views but I live in the world. I'm more than aware of the difficulties of everybody in the world with regard to having and trying to bring up children. We've somehow gone from a world in which you could have ten kids and scrape by, to a world in which four or five is a very tough thing to do. We know what is right and do our best and not judge each other. It's our job to seriously pray for each other. I wish I did more. That would be my biggest construction to making things better.

We all should argue with the Church; we're all thinking beings. God gave us brains. He doesn't want the love of slaves. He wants us to think it through and get it right.

My idea of heaven is a place where you find out everything. You

find out what's true and why it's true. Everyone's idea of heaven probably says something about them, maybe more than they know.

When you start seriously believing in God, and you believe he
set the world in motion, that indeed he breathed upon the waters
and it was good, you get an advanced appreciation of nature and of
the beauty of the non-man-made world. History is the working out
of man's fate on earth. That's an expression of God. It didn't make
me more "antiabortion"; it made me more loving about life.

About the Author

KERRY KENNEDY is the mother of three daughters: Cara, Mariah, and Michaela.

Kennedy started working in the field of human rights in 1981 when she investigated abuses committed by U.S. immigration officials against refugees from El Salvador. Since then, her life has been devoted to the vindication of equal justice, to the promotion and protection of basic rights, and to the preservation of the rule of law. She established the Robert F. Kennedy Memorial Center for Human Rights in 1988 and has worked on diverse human rights issues such as children's rights, child labor, disappearances, indigenous land rights, judicial independence, freedom of expression, ethnic violence, impunity, women's rights, and the environment. She has led over forty human rights delegations to over thirty countries.

Kennedy is the author of *Speak Truth to Power: Human Rights Defenders Who Are Changing Our World*, which features interviews with human rights activists, including Marian Wright Edelman, His Holiness, the Dalai Lama, Archbishop Desmond Tutu, Elie Wiesel, Muhammad Yunus, and others. Speak Truth to Power, a global education initiative to aid the struggle for international human rights, grew from her book exploring the quality of courage to the inspiring play by Broadway playwright Ariel Dorfman, the stirring photographic exhibition by Pulitzer Prize winner Eddie Adams, a PBS documentary film, an education packet, five public service announcements on national television, an award-winning Web site (www.speaktruthtopower.org), and federal legislation that increased federal funding for the protection of human rights.

Kennedy is chair of the Amnesty International USA Leadership Council and serves on the boards of directors of the International Center for Ethics, Justice and Public Life at Brandeis University; Human Rights First and Inter Press Service (Rome, Italy); and the Atlanta Center for Civil and Human Rights. Kennedy received high honors from President Lech Walesa of Poland for aiding the Solidarity movement. She's a member of the Massachusetts and District of Columbia bars and a graduate of Brown University and Boston College Law School.